CARING
FOR YOUR
AGING DOG

A Quality-of-Life Guide for
Your Dog's Senior Years

JANICE BORZENDOWSKI

Sterling Publishing Co., Inc.
New York

Photo Credits

Courtesy of Audrey and Joseph Anastasi, p. 71

Courtesy of Jean Beuning, Top Dog Country Club, pp. 18, 26, 50, 59, 64, 77, 86, 99, 101, 112, 114, 140, 153, 154, 165, 169, 170, 187. The Top Dog Foundation, a nonprofit organization in New Germany, Minnesota, provides sanctuary to dogs that, for reasons of age and health, are demmed unadoptable—"because every dog deserves a great life and has the right to leave this world in the arms of someone who loves them."

Courtesy of the Center for Specialized Veterinary Care, Westbury, NY, p. 121

Courtesy of April Cormaci, pp. 172, 193

Courtesy of Arnie Costell, p. 104

Courtesy of Eric Gay, p. 21

Reprinted as a courtesy, and with permission of, Doctors Foster & Smith, pp. 5, 37, 38, 146, 185

Courtesy of Terri Lonier, p. 204

Courtesy of Billy and Chris Robertazzi, pp. 45, 47

Courtesy of Renee Robertazzi, p. 40

Courtesy of Barbara Tallberg, pp. 12, 123

Library of Congress Cataloging-in-Publication Data Available

10   9   8   7   6   5   4   3   2   1

Published by Sterling Publishing Co., Inc.
387 Park Avenue South, New York, NY 10016
© 2007 by Janice Borzendowski
Distributed in Canada by Sterling Publishing
$^{C}/o$ Canadian Manda Group, 165 Dufferin Street
Toronto, Ontario, Canada M6K 3H6
Distributed in the United Kingdom by GMC Distribution Services
Castle Place, 166 High Street, Lewes, East Sussex, England BN7 1XU
Distributed in Australia by Capricorn Link (Australia) Pty. Ltd.
P.O. Box 704, Windsor, NSW 2756, Australia

Printed in China
All rights reserved

Sterling ISBN-13: 978-1-4027-2614-9
        ISBN-10: 1-4027-2614-7

For information about custom editions, special sales, premium and corporate purchases, please contact Sterling Special Sales Department at 800-805-5489 or specialsales@sterlingpub.com.

To Roy and Romo: the two best friends a girl ever had

Contents

Acknowledgments

I first must thank Dr. Richard T. Goldston, DVM, of the Parkview Animal Hospital, St. Petersburg, Florida. Called the "father of veterinary geriatrics," Dr. Goldston gave unstintingly of his expertise and materials, and his guidance and information were instrumental to the development of this book.

Thanks, also, to the other veterinarians who took time out of their busy schedules to either meet with me in person or talk with me over the phone: Dr. Josie Beug, DVM, of Five Element Animal Wellness, Miami, Florida; Dr. Grace Bransford, DVM, of the Ross Valley Veterinary Hospital, San Anselmo, California; Dr. Barbara A. Kalvig, DVM, of the New York Veterinary Hospital, New York City; Dr. Diane Levitan, VMD, of the Center for Specialized Veterinary Care, Westbury, New York; and Dr. Molly Rice, DVM, of San Francisco Veterinary Specialists, San Francisco, California.

I am very grateful, as well, to the dog lovers whose personal stories of love and care have added so much to this book: Audrey and Joseph Anastasi, April Cormaci, Arnie Costell, Terri Lonier, Renee Robertazzi, and Barbara A. Tallberg.

Next I must thank Micheline Frederick and Kerstin Nasdeo, my first readers, and two of the best editors—and the best people—I know. And to Julie Trelstad, my editor and my friend: expert at both.

Finally, to my mom, who early on instilled in me and my siblings a love of animals. I am grateful every day for that gift.

Introduction

As in many families, when it comes to remembering shared occasions or experiences, the members of my family can rarely agree. Sometimes we are even at loudly voiced odds over the most basic elements: where, when, and why—never mind who said what to whom. And we're all absolutely, positively sure we are right.

There is only one exception: the day Romo came to live with us.

Though none of us can recall the exact year, such was the effect this shepherd-collie mix had on us from the start that, to this day, we speak with a single voice when it comes to reciting the details of his arrival, one of us picking up when another leaves off. Our eyes mist over a bit; we stare back in time and smile the smile of shared joy. We grew up with many dogs, but for all of us, Romo is, and will always be, number one in our hearts.

My brother's main Christmas present that year was to be a dog, and my parents had taken him to a nearby pet store to pick one out. Mom, always a sucker for a pretty face, had lobbied hard for a purebred (a Bedlington terrier, my brother reminds me). But my brother would have none of it. He was drawn like a magnet to a forlorn-looking mixed breed, brought in the day before by a man with his son, my brother's age, who had developed an allergy to the dog. It was the last time Romo had anything but a smile on his face.

Romo's first family had named him Rommel, after the German general whose nickname was "The Desert Fox." The moniker fit perfectly. He did indeed look like a fox, with a plume for a tail, which always seemed to be wagging or waving. And he was as quick-witted as a fox; in human form he could easily have commanded an army. But my brother could not pronounce "Rommel" properly; it always came out "Romo." So Romo he became.

That first night at our house, Romo ran excitedly in circles, stopping only for the briefest of seconds to bestow slobbering wet kisses on everyone—including the cat, who was clearly insulted by the tongue splashing, but was too nonplussed to muster up a hiss or a swat. It was like watching happiness on the run, and it was infectious. Soon we were all laughing with abandon.

Though officially my brother's, Romo was truly the family dog. More accurately, we were his charges. Ostensibly, we took care of him, but food, a home, and the odd trip to the vet were insubstantial compared to the experience of being sheltered under the watchful eye of Romo. He was our great companion, and in the days before the dog leash law went into effect in our still-small southwestern city, Romo went everywhere with us. Sometimes, such as when our family went to the strip mall to run errands, Romo had a big decision to make. Using his own criteria (which we never figured out), Romo would choose which of us was to be the "anchor person" that day. Wherever that person went—the grocery store, the toy store, or the drugstore—he followed, then assumed his post outside. From there, ever vigilant, he'd keep his eye on the other locations where "his people" had gone. He was so good-natured and well-behaved that shoppers coming and going always stopped to give him a pat or a scratch, followed by the inevitable, "What a good dog." He basked in the attention, passing on love and goodwill the way people pass on a cold: you couldn't not catch it.

In those days, during the hot summers, after school had let out for the year, Romo, my brother, and I took to the desert. There was a lot to explore, and we did our best to upturn every stone, poke in every puddle, and dig in every crack and crevice in the rocky, cactus-dotted landscape. Romo was our scout. He unearthed lizards and snakes, jackrabbits and roadrunners to show us all the interesting creatures of our environment. He could run like the wind and gave many a wild animal a run for its life. But he always doubled back within what he considered a reasonable time, tongue lolling, tail pointing the direction of the breeze. He'd check on us, and see what we were up to; if it wasn't all that interesting to him, off he'd go again. He wasn't afraid of much, or anything as far as we could determine, and he taught us to be curious, daring, adventurous. No small gifts.

Looking back, I know Romo had a happy life. And for the most part he was healthy. But now I wonder if that was due to his good genes or our good luck. Back then pet care was not something much talked or written about. There were no community spay/neuter campaigns that I can recall; pet superstores, with their long, tall aisles of products and information, were still a few years away; and pet carelessness, not pet care, was the norm when most dogs were allowed to roam free. Romo was vaccinated, of course, and wore the jewelry to prove it. But it was probably the only preventive measure we took to ensure his health. Otherwise, he was taken to the vet only for serious matters or in an emergency. Of the times he required emergency care, the visit that stands out in my mind came after one of his famous desert chases, in this case for a jackrabbit. He refused to give up even after the jackrabbit had taken refuge under a chollo cactus (nicknamed, appropriately, "jumping cactus"). That day, the vet needed all his strength and a serious-looking pair of pliers to extract the fearsome, spiny needles from poor Romo's nose. But he was good to go again by the next day.

By the time Romo became a "senior," we were all grown and spending less time hanging out with him. I don't think we even noticed he was getting old; certainly he didn't mention it. And even if we had noticed, as far as we knew there was no such thing as specialized veterinary care for senior pets. Romo spent his "golden years" mostly inside, where it was cool, exploring only the backyard when some scent on the wind stirred up memories of past wanderings.

It was some eighteen years after that first boisterous night in our house, and after my sister, brother, and I had all moved away from home, that my mother, alone, bore the task of taking Romo, who could no longer hear, see clearly, or stand up unassisted, to be euthanized. I know she cried; but I don't remember if I did when I heard—I was miles and time away. I'm crying now, though. I miss my old friend.

If Romo were alive today, he'd be treated by veterinarians who know more about small-animal geriatrics than ever before in history. This rapidly growing field of veterinary medicine makes it possible for our dogs to live not just longer lives, but to live long lives of quality. And it's not just the science and technology that's changing health care for our pets; it's knowledge about the effects of proper nutrition and exercise on the life of our dogs. We even know more about dog psychology, and about the effects of old age on a dog's brain. In short, we can finally return the age-old favor and become dog's best friend. This book will help you learn how to do that. They deserve it.

RETURNING THE FAVOR

Caring for an aging dog is not all that different from caring for our own bodies as we go through the various stages of life. A lot of it is common sense, coupled with awareness. When it comes to our own health care, we all know we should go regularly to the dentist to have a checkup and get our teeth cleaned; likewise, we're aware we should have a yearly physical exam, to serve as a baseline of numerous health indicators; we also know the dangers of obesity, and the importance of proper nutrition and exercise to maintaining a healthy weight; and we've been told to watch for the warning signs of various types of cancer, hypertension, diabetes, and countless other diseases and conditions. Some of us are better than others at following through on the medical advice and information we receive; and whether we do or don't is our choice. But our dogs have no choice: they're entirely dependent on us for ensuring they receive the proper care and the best chance of a long, healthy life.

Today, plenty of help is available for our aging dogs. Advances in veterinary medicine have nearly matched in speed and number those in human medicine. You simply have to learn what's available and how to go about implementing what you learn. This book is set up to guide you through an effective approach to caring for your aging dog.

Part 1, "Understanding the Life of an Older Dog," is designed to introduce the basics of caring for your senior dog, beginning with figuring out how old he actually is (you might be surprised), followed by a prevention primer, which is all-important to ensuring quality of life for as long as your dog lives.

- In Chapter 1, "A Year in the Life of a Dog," you'll learn how to calculate your dog's actual age—not in human terms, but in "dog years"—and how those years translate to changes in your dog's health. (Hint: You don't just multiply by seven.) You'll also learn the "big three" factors contributing to how a dog ages: genetics, environment, and nutrition.
- In Chapter 2, "Prevention: Taking a Proactive Approach to Caring for Your Dog," I'll explain how you can forestall the onset of disease and old-age conditions, or lessen their impact, by following four simple guidelines: pay attention, schedule

biannual checkups, plan ahead, and trust your instincts. You'll be introduced to the senior wellness program and its importance to your dog's health, today and tomorrow.

- In Chapter 3, "Vital Signs: Recognizing Signals of Change from Your Dog," we'll look at both physical and mental signs of your dog's aging body, from cloudy eyes and achy joints to bad breath and weird behavior, and everything in between.

Part 2, "Geriatric Canine Health Care," gets down to the more complicated business of understanding the diseases and ailments a typical aging dog—and you, his owner—may face. The better informed you are about the diseases and disorders associated with the aging dog, the better able you'll be to help provide the care he needs. You are an integral member of your dog's health care team, and his first line of defense.

- In Chapter 4, "Wellness Programs: Keeping Your Dog Healthy for the Long Term," you'll find out why the geriatric veterinary community prefers to use the term "wellness" when referring to a lifetime of health care for your dog. We'll go into some detail as to the makeup of a standard wellness exam and program, so that you understand fully why it is necessary and how it helps both you and your vet provide your dog with optimum care. But first we'll discuss how to find a veterinarian or evaluate your current vet.
- In Chapter 5, "Nutrition, Exercise, and Grooming: Keeping Your Dog in Shape," you'll find out why it's so important to feed your dog properly; exercise him, both mentally and physically; and groom him from nose to toes (grooming, you may be surprised to learn, is a vital factor in maintaining an aging dog's health).
- Chapter 6, "When Your Dog Gets Sick: Understanding Common Age-Related Ailments and Their Treatments," is a primer intended to familiarize you with many of the most

common diseases of older dogs. You'll read about treatment options, too, including alternative choices.

- Chapter 7, "Dollar Signs: Managing the Costs of Senior Pet Care," addresses the dreaded question: How much is this going to cost me? We'll talk about health insurance, cost-savings programs, and other options for addressing the bottom line.

Part 3, "Quality-of-Life and End-of-Life Issues," helps you face what you may have trouble acknowledging: that you and your dog are coming to the end of your days together.

- In Chapter 8, "Quality of Life: Answering the Hard Questions," we'll address such questions as: How can I tell when my dog is in pain or discomfort? What constitutes quality of life for a dog? We'll talk, too, about your quality of life as it relates to caring for your dog, so that you can safely ride the emotional rollercoaster of worry, fear, guilt, and so on.
- Chapter 9, "Farewell Friend: Coming to Terms with End of Life," helps you face the inevitable: the death of your dog. We'll talk about hospice care for your dog, as important a concept in geriatric pet care as it is in human health care, as well as how to prepare yourself and your family. We'll discuss the difficult topics of euthanasia and "aftercare" (burial versus cremation). Finally, you'll learn how and where to find support for you (and your family) during the first difficult days and weeks of coping with the loss of your best friend. Some pet owners are surprised at how deeply affected they are, and for how long, by the death of their dog.
- In the Epilogue, we'll broach the subject of moving forward after the death of your dog, and how that might happen for you.

Throughout the book, you'll also find personal stories from pet owners who have "been there, done that," or are doing it right now—caring for a beloved older dog. You'll be inspired by their efforts and their devotion, and learn from their experiences. Also interspersed throughout the text are sidebars of special or related interest to the subject at hand; "Who's Who" entries defining pet care groups, organizations, and other resources; and other notes, tips, and items of interest. Each chapter ends with "Key Pet Points," to summarize the important "takeaway" concepts from each chapter.

The key point I would like you to take away from this introduction is that you can begin the process of caring for your older dog by keeping your heart open to the possibility that it will come to mean much more than trips to the vet, a struggle to give medications, the cost to your budget and your peace of mind, and the inevitable disruption to your normal routine. The opportunity to care in this way is a gift, one I believe you will come to cherish.

PART 1

Understanding the Life of an Older Dog

CHAPTER 1

A Year in the Life of a Dog

While heading back from a walk on the beach near my sister's house in northern California, I crossed paths with a pug named Danny. The narrow sidewalk made introductions unavoidable—though, as is often the case in these situations, only the dog was introduced. As I knelt to respond to Danny's demand for attention, his owner announced proudly that they had just celebrated his fifth birthday, the day before, on St. Patrick's Day. Danny seemed unaware of the momentousness of the occasion, especially as he was busy sniffing my shoes and pant cuffs, undoubtedly while sorting through his scent database to determine whether he recognized the smell of my sister's dog. As we went our separate ways, I smiled at the image of Danny in a typical paper birthday hat, akimbo on his head and secured under his chin, and wondered if there had been brightly colored birthday bones, topped with five candles.

Danny's owner has a lot of company: thousands of pet owners in this country celebrate their pet's birthday (various surveys estimate between 43 and 70 percent of 65 million owned dogs). That's a lot of people buying presents for and/or preparing a special meal to commemorate their dog's birthday. So it's safe to say that most pet owners know how old their dogs are. But do they know how those years translate into changes in their dog's health? Counting the years is not the same as recognizing the effects of those years on a dog's body, and understanding those effects is the first step in learning to care for your aging dog.

Landmark Birthday

The oldest dog on record was 29. The average lifespan of all dog breeds is around 13.5 years.

When it comes to our own aging process, we humans are acutely aware of every change, real or imagined. Our culture is so age conscious that we're bombarded constantly with innumerable products and services that promise to slow, or at least hide, the aging process. We prowl the increasingly long and complex aisles in the drugstore, looking for cosmetics of mass denial; we note every ache and pain, wrinkle and gray hair; and we waste no time in seeking advice and remedies from doctors who specialize in safeguarding even the most remote regions of our bodies from the hands of time.

We're much less attuned to our dog's aging process, however. According to Dr. Richard Goldston, DVM, ACVIM, known as the father of veterinary geriatrics, "the most common mistake people make in evaluating the health of their pets is to assume the problems or signs they see as abnormal in their pets are due to 'just getting old.' When this mistake is made, the pet is frequently not presented to the family veterinarian for a more thorough evaluation."

Vets from around the country concur. Dr. Josie Beug, DVM, a veterinary acupuncturist in Miami, Florida, says, "The biggest mistake is denial, and waiting too long." (She adds that anthropomorphizing, or attributing human characteristics to an animal's behavior, is another common mistake.) Dr. Molly Rice, DVM, on the staff at San Francisco Veterinary Specialists, echoes Dr. Beug, saying simply: "Waiting too long to seek treatment is the biggest mistake."

It's all too easy to make that mistake, however, because, of course, dogs don't complain in "human speak," so you might not notice for some time that Barney Basset has been slow to greet you when you come home from work (if he makes it to the door at all); or doesn't

GUS'S STORY: PAYING ATTENTION TO THE SIGNS OF AGING

Gus is a pound puppy we took home on a trial basis more than ten years ago—"trial" because we weren't sure how our older dog (also a Pekingese) would accept him. He easily won over this feisty and finicky female,

Gus, aka "Funny Face"

earning him the nickname "Funny Face" in the process, for all his delightful antics and effervescent vitality. The veterinarians could only guess he was around four years old at the time.

Over the years, Gus trained us well. He taught us that car rides are the stuff of magic. He is particularly fond of trips to our neighborhood drive-through espresso shop, where he learned quickly that if he barked in various tones and bobbed his head back and forth, he would get a doggie treat. He even developed a "thank-you" bark.

But his favorite activity is to go out for a walk after eating. In his early years with us, he would demonstrate it was time to head out by nuzzling our feet and then placing a paw on top of one of them to indicate it was time to put on our shoes. But over the last year or so, his nuzzling had become less frequent, the walks shorter. My husband and I wrote it off to Gus "just not feeling like a walk," and didn't give it much thought beyond that. After all, he would still chase Skittles, the calico cat across the street, so we ignored these signs.

Then, in early December Gus and I were playing "sock." He particularly liked the stretchy nylon ones because he could hold down one end while pulling taut the other end with his teeth. This day, however, although his exuberance carried his front quarters sharply around a corner (sock in mouth), his hind legs failed to make the turn. I heard a loud yelp of pain. By the time I reached him, Gus was spread out, with his front half on one side of the wall, his backside on the other. His sock was forgotten, and the look of shock and fear was clear in his normally bright eyes.

We took Gus to our local veterinarian, who identified a spinal injury. At that time he could only wobble on his front legs, while his rear quarters splayed out like lumps of soft dough. You could feel the heat radiating from his midback, which I later learned was the T-L junction. The diagnosis was something called intervertebral disk disease, IVDD. Our vet put him on a steroid, prednisone, two times a day. But it seemed to me he was suffering even with the drug, and his quality of life was now dramatically reduced. He depended entirely on me for survival. Over-night I had become his legs, carrying him up and down the stairs, making sure he had water bowls in strategic locations, and keeping him as immobile as possible in order for his injury to heal.

Several weeks went by as I watched him become less active and more needy. His eyes became cloudy, and the only time he became animated was when he thought food might be involved. I learned that one of the side effects of prednisone is an increased appetite—hardly desirable for an animal that was in an almost vegetative state. He would inhale any food put in his bowl, and then of course become nauseous because he had eaten so quickly.

I found myself raising my voice to get him to eat more slowly. He could only look at me with sad, misty eyes and tilt his head as if to say, "I'm sorry, I can't help it." Then I'd start crying, holding him close, because I had lost my patience. I began to dread the feeding routine, which had ironically become one of his favorite times. And I fantasized about installing tile flooring, because that would be easier to clean, and then immediately felt guilty because that would be more difficult for Gus to walk on. I seemed to have no control over the situation or what was happening to my formerly happy, vital dog.

My days began to revolve around making sure Gus's needs were met. Did I give him his pills? Were his numerous water bowls filled? Was it time to pick him up and carry him outside? Was it raining out? Did he need to go—fast? At some point I became aware that if I addressed my needs before feeding him, I was much more comfortable taking him out immediately after he had eaten. That was probably my first step toward defining a balance between his needs and mine.

Walking with Gus on a particularly brilliant morning, watching him valiantly and with great concentration attempt to place one paw in front of the other, I discovered that he was teaching me a life lesson, even in all his discomfort. I was learning, really integrating at some cellular level, that it doesn't matter how long it takes to move forward, so long as you keep moving. Every little wobbly step is important, even if you trip and fall in the process. Time and again, with great dignity and resolve, Gus would right himself and proceed in his effort to move forward. He didn't complain or blame anyone for his accident or the circumstances he found himself in.

A few months later, an auspicious phone conversation would change Gus's stumbling ways.

—*Barbara Tallberg, Northern California*

Read the conclusion of Gus's story in Chapter 6. (It has a happy ending.)

---

have his old "get up and go" when you jangle the leash, signaling it's time for a walk; or just pushes his food around in the dish with his nose. Sadly, that could also mean that Barney isn't getting the care he needs to ensure he has a long and healthy life.

How can you avoid making this mistake with your best friend? We'll talk more about this in Chapter 3, "Vital Signs: Recognizing Signals of Change from Your Dog." First, though, you need to figure out how old your dog really is—in dog years.

Who's Who in Pet Health Care: The American Animal Hospital Association (AAHA)

The more than thirty-two thousand members of the American Animal Hospital Association work primarily in the health care of companion animals. These professionals include everyone you'll find in a veterinary clinic, hospital, or office: veterinarians, technicians, managers, receptionists, and others. The AAHA's motto is "Healthy Practices, Healthier Pets." The AAHA Web site is primarily designed for veterinary professionals, but a layperson can learn a lot from a visit there. Go to: www.aahanet.org.

Understanding Old Is New . . .

In the past, veterinary health care programs were divided into two categories: young and adult (as opposed to "old") animals. The former involved shots for the pediatric group, followed by booster vaccines for rabies, heartworm, flea control, and so on for adult dogs. Recognition came gradually about the different care requirements for older pets—interestingly, as an outgrowth of early studies of human geriatrics—as a distinct field of medical care.

Early on, statements about human geriatric work were applied directly to dogs only (not cats). But, says Dr. Richard Goldston, as specialization in veterinary medicine grew, research in specific organ functions–such as kidney, liver, and heart–"suggested" that older pets might need different levels of medications, since the older dog might not be able to metabolize, or excrete, the normal doses of drugs as effectively as younger animals can.

In 1984, Dr. Goldston established a geriatric wellness program in his private practice and began giving lectures and writing articles on geriatric disorders of dogs and cats. Recognizing his growing expertise, a professional publisher asked him to compile the first comprehensive textbook specifically on the geriatrics of the dog and cat. The result, in 1995, was the publication of *Geriatrics and Gerontology of the Dog and Cat* (W.B. Saunders & Co., now Elsevier), co-edited with Dr. Johnny Hoskins of Louisiana State University College of Veterinary Medicine.

As a consequence of this groundbreaking publication, veterinary medicine began viewing geriatrics as a distinct "wellness" area, leading to the development of geriatric-specific foods, medicines, diets, and comprehensive health care programs. Soon, geriatrics became, as Dr. Goldston puts it, "the next wave in veterinary medicine across the country and in institutional and industry studies." But as recently as 1999, small-animal geriatrics was still considered an emerging market.

A walk down the aisles of any pet superstore today would seem to leave no question that it has fully arrived.

Geriatric dogs and cats now comprise the largest caseload percentage in most veterinary practices and hospitals across the country, and veterinary schools routinely offer training in geriatrics.

CALCULATING THE AGE OF YOUR DOG

Most of us learned that the way to determine a dog's age was to multiply his actual age by seven. That's one of those bits of misinformation that has, over time, acquired the ring of truth—in no small part because it's so easy to remember and has been repeated so many times. But it's not really an accurate way to "date your dog"—though it does serve to make the point that dogs age a lot more quickly than we do. And seven *is* an important number in a dog's life, because it's the age at which most vets consider dogs to be at the beginning of old age. But keep in mind it's an average; the aging process varies by size and breed, nutrition, environment, and other factors. So variable is the aging calculation, in fact, that the American Animal Hospital Association (AAHA) prefers to use instead what's called an *end-of-lifespan percentage*. The association's 2005 "Senior Care Guidelines for Dogs and Cats" recommends that its practitioners apply the guidelines to those animals that are in the last 25 percent of their predicted lifespan for the species and breed.

In addition, it's important to recognize three primary factors that impact aging in your dog:

• Genetics
• Environment
• Nutrition

The Gene Factor

To determine when you need to start seeking senior care for your dog, you first have to figure out whether he's considered a "senior" (old) or a "geriatric" (very old). Though breed does play a role in aging, it appears to be a much less important one than size/weight, so the first step is to find out how much your dog weighs. A quick call to your vet's office will give you this number—if your dog had a checkup recently. If not, and your dog is a manageable size, you can put him on your own scale at home to get a reasonable estimate. If you have a large- or giant-size dog, you might be able to get him weighed at one of the pet superstores, such as PETCO or PetSmart.

As a baseline, small dogs (less than 20 pounds) are considered geriatric at nine years; medium dogs (21–50 pounds) at eight years; large

---

Breed Right

Breed can become as important a factor in life expectancy—if not more so—as size, depending on the breeder you use. Disreputable breeders often resort to the practice of inbreeding, the interbreeding of closely related individuals (e.g., mothers and sons, sisters and brothers, etc.) for the purpose of preserving and fixing desirable characteristics and/or to eliminate unfavorable characteristics—such as length of ear, height of leg, coat color, and many others. However, the practice also can result in a heightened tendency to develop either behavioral or physical dysfunctions. That is why, in general, mixed-breed dogs—mutts—live longer than their purebred counterparts. To find out the estimated life expectancy of your purebred dog, and for more on breeders and breeding, go to the American Kennel Club's Web site, www.akc.org.

HOW OLD IS YOUR DOG?

Dog's Age	Human-Equivalent Years (based on weight, in pounds)			
	0–20	21–50	51–90	>90
5	36	37	40	42
6	40	42	45	49
7	44	47	50	56
8	48	51	55	64
9	52	56	61	71
10	56	60	66	78
11	60	65	72	86
12	64	69	77	93
13	68	74	82	101
14	72	78	88	108
15	76	83	93	115
16	80	87	99	123
17	84	92	104	
18	88	96	109	
19	92	101	115	
20	96	105	120	

Key: Senior   Geriatric

Source: Based on a chart developed by Fred L. Metzger, DVM; adapted by William Fortney, DVM, R. T. Goldston, DVM, and Ernest Ward Jr., DVM. Reprinted with permission of Dr. Goldston.

dogs (51–90 pounds) at seven years; and giant breeds (more than 91 pounds) at six years. For a more specific breakdown of the age-weight relationship, take a look at the table "How Old Is Your Dog?"

In terms of longevity, size really matters. One study reported that only 13 percent of giant breeds lived past ten years, and of those only 0.1 percent lived to be fifteen. In comparison, 38 percent of small breeds lived to be ten, and 7 percent lived to fifteen and older.

When it comes to breed, what are called "longevity genes" also come into play in other ways than adult size—though, as in humans, it is not clear why. For example, no one can really explain why someone who smokes three packs of cigarettes a day all his life lives to ninety, defying the odds. In the dog world, collies and boxers, for example, seem to be missing the longevity gene: they tend to have shorter life expectancies even when size is taken into consideration. And mixed breeds generally live longer than purebreds due to what's referred to as "hybrid vigor."

Who's Who in Pet Health Care: The American Kennel Club (AKC)

The AKC, founded in 1884 by a group of twelve sportsmen, today states as its threefold mission to: "maintain a registry for purebred dogs and preserve its integrity [it reports parentage of more than 1 million dogs annually]; sanction dog events that promote interest in, and sustain the process of, breeding for type and function of purebred dogs [annually, it sponsors more than fifteen thousand dog competitions]; take whatever actions necessary to protect and assure the continuation of the sport of purebred dogs."

The Environmental Effect

Where your dog lives also has a lot to do with how long he'll live. Is your dog a city canine, confined to an apartment most of the time except for two or three walks daily and a romp in the park a couple of times a week? Is your dog a suburbanite, living indoors much of the time but with access to a yard, where he's free to prowl part of the day? Or is your dog a rural roamer, unconfined and outdoors most of the time? Dr. Barbara Kalvig, DVM, medical director for the New York Veterinary Hospital, says that environment and how pet owners treat their pets are major factors in how quickly dogs age. She sees a big difference between city dwellers, where people are "really connected" to their dogs (and who, for example, see their dogs' stools on a daily basis and note changes almost immediately), as opposed to suburban or rural inhabitants whose dogs are just let out in the yard and are not monitored as closely.

Rural versus urban veterinary care also is part of the environmental equation. In general, urban pets may receive better care simply because pet owners in larger municipalities have access to the full range of veterinary specialists—including board-certified internists, surgeons, ophthalmologists, dermatologists, dentists, behaviorists, oncologists, holistic practitioners, and more. Rural communities generally cannot support this advanced level of care and technology.

Environment is an issue, as well, when it comes to your dog's health care program. City dogs, for example, are exposed to many more parasites and infections, and so may require more frequent vaccinations than, say, suburban canines.

Nutrition: Taking Care of the Inner Dog

Dogs may not "be what they eat," but there's no question that what they eat has a marked impact on their life expectancy and quality of life. Now, thanks to advances in research and a deeper understanding of how dogs digest and process food, feeding a dog properly should

Pet-Healthy Cities

When it comes to choosing where we live, most of us follow a job opportunity, a spouse, a climate, or a culture. If our pets could choose, they might follow their nose to one of the "pet-healthiest cities," as determined from a survey conducted in 2005 by the Purina Pet Institute's Healthy Pets 21 Consortium, in conjunction with demographic consultant Bert Sperling (who collects and analyzes the data for *Money* magazine's annual Best Places to Live). Using twenty-three criteria in three categories–health, services, and legislation–the institute compiled the first-ever list of the fifty pet-healthiest cities in the United States. The top five are:

1. Denver, Colorado
2. Minneapolis, Minnesota
3. Columbus, Ohio
4. Philadelphia, Pennsylvania
5. Seattle, Washington

What do these locales have that others don't? According to the consortium, they all scored high in meeting such criteria as high vet-to-pet ratios (Denver boasts one vet for every twelve hundred pets), number of affiliated staff at accredited veterinary hospitals, number of veterinary surgeons, access to emergency veterinary care, number of certified shelters, appropriate rabies vaccination and pet identification requirements, licensing fee reductions for spayed/neutered pets, and cruelty investigation programs.

Other cities making the list (and their rank) include: San Francisco (8); Los Angeles (13); Boston (17); Chicago (18); New York City (35); Cincinnati (42); and Miami (50).

Curious whether your city was one of the fifty? Go to www.purina.com/institute, where you can view the entire list, learn how to make your community healthier for pets, and read more about the work of the consortium.

be no problem. But it still can be. Why? Because in tandem with greater knowledge in the field of animal nutrition has come an almost mind-boggling range of pet foods. Trolling the aisles of your favorite pet supply or grocery store, you've no doubt been amazed—if not overwhelmed—by the myriad brands and types of dog food now on the shelves. In bags and boxes, cans and pouches, cartons and other distinctive containers, seemingly, there's a flavor and diet suitable for dogs of every size, shape, age, and physical condition. But are they as suitable as they promise? How do you know and how do you choose?

Just by asking those questions, you're on the right path to finding the appropriate food(s) for your senior dog. Now is the right time to reevaluate your dog's diet, in consultation with your vet and as part of his regular checkups. In Chapters 4 and 5 we'll talk more about dog food, and how to be sure your dog is on the right diet for his age and health status. For now, be aware that obese dogs have shorter life expectancies than those kept at or near their ideal weight. And animals maintained strictly on high-quality balanced commercial diets live longer than animals fed table scraps or cheaper brands of dog food—high-fat and/or low-fiber diets decrease life expectancy. Sound familiar?

SUMMARY

It's never too late to start giving your older dog the care he needs, but sooner is definitely better. To that end, be alert to signs that changes are taking place in your dog's body and behavior, and address them promptly with your vet. The best chance your dog has for a long and healthy life depends on your attentiveness. Now's the time to start repaying all that unconditional love. In the next chapter, we begin by learning to read vital signs your dog may be sending you.

KEY PET POINTS

- As accurately as possible, estimate your dog's age, in dog years. If you don't know when he was born, ask your vet to help determine his age.

- Understand the importance of size/weight—and, to a lesser extent, breed—on canine longevity.

- Recognize that your environment affects your dog's health much as it does your own.

- It may be easier, more convenient, and less expensive to grab your grocery store's generic-brand dog food off the shelf. But do you know what's in there? It could, over time, seriously impact your dog's well-being. Good nutrition is not just for humans anymore.

CHAPTER 2

Prevention: Taking a Proactive Approach to Caring for Your Dog

Taking preventive measures for the care of your dog is the best way to ensure quality of life for her, for as long as possible. Even in the best-case scenario, the age-related changes your dog will inevitably experience may cause major disruptions to your life, on practical, psychological, and emotional levels. By being prepared, you stand the best chance for doing right by your dog—and yourself.

This chapter offers four guidelines that, taken together, can form an effective strategy for caring for your aging or geriatric dog:

1. Pay attention.
2. Schedule biannual checkups.
3. Plan ahead.
4. Trust your instincts.

PAY ATTENTION

As we all know from trying to multitask our way through our busy lives, rarely these days do we truly give anything the attention it deserves. But if you'll let her, your dog can make caring for her in her senior years not just easy, but a real pleasure. Unlike their less fortunate human companions, dogs have never lost the ability to live in the moment. They're always right there, and would love it if you joined them. If you're a city dweller, for example, when you walk your dog, instead of talking on your cell phone at the same

time (or reading the paper or planning dinner or concentrating on any of a thousand distractions), *really* walk your dog: take pleasure in her pleasure as she relishes every new scent, chases every falling leaf or squirrel, and introduces herself to all and sundry she meets along the way. If you live in a house with a yard, instead of just opening the door and letting your dog out, then reading the mail or starting dinner, walk outside with her—*be* with her. When you do that on a daily basis, you won't fail to notice changes—even subtle ones—in her body and behavior.

The point is, your dog isn't going to leave you a note or send you an e-mail telling you it's time to make an appointment with her vet. But she can, and will, give you signs. It's up to you to recognize them. You may not know exactly how to interpret these signs—

Good for You, Too

By spending "quality time" with your dog, you might be pleasantly surprised at the benefits to you, in the form of stress reduction and renewed focus on the important things in life.

that's what your dog's veterinarian is for—but unless you're paying attention, you'll pass them by on the way to grab another cup of coffee and miss the first, and best, chance you have to give your dog the care she needs. Dr. Grace Bransford of the Ross Valley Clinic in San Anselmo, California, says the biggest mistake pet owners make in caring for their dogs is "not seeing." Not seeing comes from not paying attention.

To give you a head start on learning to read "sign language," take a look at the checklist titled "Signs Your Dog Is Getting Old," on page 28. Maybe you're already aware—even if only vaguely—of some of these signs; if so, check 'em off as a way to bring focus to them. If nothing rings a bell yet, consider yourself lucky; but keep these signs in mind (better yet, make a copy of this list and keep it handy) so that you're prepared to make note of them and pass the information on to your vet. This list is by no means comprehensive; and every dog is different, so jot down anything and everything in your dog's behavior or demeanor that strikes you as "not right."

In Chapter 3, "Vital Signs: Recognizing Signals of Change from Your Dog," you'll learn more about what these and other signs might mean. For now just be aware that keeping a list like this up to date will be valuable down the road, for three important purposes:

- You will be better prepared to help your vet help your dog.
- You will have an easier time understanding the objectives of the screening exams your vet will conduct.
- You will more fully understand the reasoning behind treatments or lifestyle adjustments (including nutrition, exercise, and grooming) your vet may recommend for your dog.

And that leads us to the second guideline: taking your dog in for regular checkups.

SIGNS YOUR DOG IS GETTING OLD

Sign	Yes	No
Difficulty climbing stairs?		
Difficulty jumping up?		
Increased stiffness or limping?		
Incontinence?		
Increased thirst?		
Increased urination?		
Straining while defecating?		
Change in activity level?		
Excessive panting or change in breathing?		
Circling or repetitive movements?		
Confusion or disorientation?		
Excessive barking/whining?		
Less interaction with family? Hiding?		
Decreased responsiveness?		
Tremors or shaking?		
Skin and hair coat changes?		
Lumps or bumps?		
Excessive scratching?		
Changes in sleeping patterns/locations?		
Less enthusiastic greeting behavior?		
Altered appetite?		
Weight change (up or down)?		
Vomiting or diarrhea?		
Bad breath?		
Other?		

Source: Adapted with permission from William Fortney, DVM.

Top Priority

Though too few pet owners of older dogs follow the twice-a-year checkup recommendation, overall most say they are more likely to take better care of their dog's health than they are their own. According to a pet owner survey conducted in 2004 by the AAHA, 58 percent of some 1,238 pet owners surveyed in more than 160 accredited veterinary practices said they visit their pet's veterinarian more often than their own physician. More interesting still is that 93 percent said they are likely to risk their own life for their pet.

SCHEDULE BIANNUAL CHECKUPS

Even if you've noticed no signs so far that your dog is experiencing age-related health changes, that doesn't mean she isn't. Many, maybe most, are not apparent to the naked eye. That's why veterinarians are unanimous in their conviction that a biannual checkup for aging dogs—beginning at the magic number seven—is the *single best way* to keep your dog well cared for throughout her senior and geriatric years. I know, I know: it's a miracle when you remember to schedule an appointment once a year for your own annual checkup. But, says Dr. Goldston, "No health care program is more important in maintaining and prolonging a high-quality life for the pet, while meeting the most important needs of the owner, than a thorough geriatrics wellness program that is carried out to the fullest." Note what he said about meeting *your* needs, too: imagine your life without your dog. Their years with us are too short as it is, and taking this step can help to extend the years we spend with them.

Sad to say, though, too many of us fail to take this important step. According to the AAHA's "Senior Care Guidelines," only some 14 percent of senior animals are taken for the checkups recommended by their veterinarians.

Why is this twice-a-year checkup so important to your dog?

Three important reasons: first, it enables the early detection of abnormalities; which, second, makes it possible for your vet to design an individualized health care program for your dog; and third, it allows your vet to establish baseline data about your dog's health, which he or she will use subsequently to compare against information gathered at future checkups. According to the AAHA's "Senior Care Guidelines," "A wealth of scientific literature documents the presence of subclinical disease [meaning the disease is present but not yet causing external symptoms] in some healthy-appearing animals; to illuminate such conditions, there is no substitute for a thorough and complete history and physical examination. In addition, subtle changes in laboratory test results may give an indication of the presence of underlying disease." With early detection—and thanks to the numerous advances being made every day in veterinary medicine—it is often possible to postpone, or minimize, the effects of those changes, sometimes for years. Moreover, taking preventive measures may spare you costly treatments down the road. Isn't that worth taking out your calendar and scheduling two appointments now? As Dr. Goldston says, "This geriatric wellness program is good for our patients, it's good for our clients, and it's good for our hospitals."

Tip

If you celebrate your dog's birthday, what better way than to schedule one checkup on that date and the second six months away? Also, find out whether your vet sends out reminder cards, to help you follow through.

The Geriatric Wellness Program: Short Version

The objective in this section is to give you an overview within the broader context of prevention. Chapter 4, "Wellness Programs: Keeping Your Dog Healthy for the Long Term," details the various components of a typical geriatric wellness workup.

Beginning when your dog enters her geriatric years, this program should continue through her "golden" years. For you, it will involve discussions of and decisions regarding medical treatments, terminal illness, and, eventually, death (natural or by euthanasia). Ideally, says Dr. Goldston, the program will also include the handling of your pet's remains, your grief process (including bereavement counseling), and, possibly, welcoming a new dog into your life.

For your dog, the program will involve a number of elements. Briefly:

Physical exam: Includes a check of your dog's general appearance; temperature, pulse, and respiration (TPR); body weight; heart and lungs; ears, eyes, and teeth; thyroid glands; and skin.

Complete blood test: Helps to diagnose infection, anemia, bleeding problems, and cancer. Also gives insight into your dog's immune system.

Serum chemistry profile: Assesses function of liver, kidneys, pancreas, and other organs.

Complete urinalysis: Assesses kidney function and reveals infection.

Fecal analysis: Checks for evidence of parasites and unusual bacteria and protozoa; evaluates red and white blood cells.

On an individual basis, as necessary, your vet may recommend other tests, such as:

- Radiography
- Echocardiography
- Abdominal ultrasonography
- Thyroid and adrenal gland testing
- Blood pressure measurement
- Other organ function tests

What, you might ask, is the point of doing all these tests on an old dog? As stated previously, early detection enables more effective

Test Preparation

Before doing any additional testing, your vet should explain to you the purpose of the test, why he or she thinks it is necessary (what, exactly, he or she is looking for), and how much it will cost. Your vet should ask you for permission to proceed with the additional work.

treatment. Even those diseases and disorders that are incurable from the outset can be controlled and managed, if major tissue or organ damage has not yet occurred, says Dr. Goldston. The bottom line for your dog: longer life, at a higher quality. The bottom line for you: more valuable time with your best friend.

PLAN AHEAD

Everything we've been talking about so far could probably fall under this heading. But in this section, I want to address day-to-day life with a geriatric dog, for a great deal of what happens to an aging animal falls in the realm of the unexpected. Your dog is not likely to become bloated (a serious condition in dogs, which you'll learn about in Chapter 6), have a seizure, or fall down the stairs on cue, the very day she is scheduled to go to the vet. No, it will probably happen in the middle of the night, late on a Sunday afternoon, or when you're out of town on business and your dog is in the care of a pet sitter. Now what? These situations are never pleasant or easy, but how well you have planned for the unexpected will, to some degree, dictate the outcome. Here are some guidelines for making the best of a bad situation.

Prepare for Emergencies

No matter how conscientious you are, no matter how carefully you pay attention and take all the proper precautions, your geriatric dog is going to present you with some challenging, even daunting, moments. Few of us are at our best at such times; many of us become unglued, especially when a loved one is in danger or pain. To ensure that cooler heads prevail when your dog is in trouble, take these precautions:

Have names and numbers handy. Post them on the refrigerator, on the side of the computer monitor, or wherever your go-to spot is in your home. The names and numbers you should include:

- Your veterinarian
- The nearest emergency services veterinary hospital or clinic (preferably a twenty-four-hour facility)
- Poison control center or hotline

Help! My Dog Just Ate Something . . .

Add this number to your list: 888-426-4435. It is the ASPCA Animal Poison Control Center, in Urbana, Illinois, which is staffed by veterinary toxicologists. Take your credit card out before you call, as there's a consultation fee–around $50.

Keep your dog's medical paperwork handy. Maintain a file of your dog's vaccinations, medications, and other medical records; keep it up to date and easily accessible. In an emergency, remember, you may not be seeing your dog's regular vet, and you'll want to provide the alternate veterinarian with as much background information as possible.

Learn some basic first-aid/emergency procedures. You may find yourself in the unenviable position of having to act now and call for help later. Maybe your dog fractured a limb, is choking, or is bleeding. Knowing basic first aid could save your dog's life. It's a good idea to purchase one of the numerous first-aid books for dogs that are now available. Ask your vet to recommend a good one—and to step through the procedures with you, if you're not comfortable performing first aid on your dog. To get an idea of what such books contain, go online and check out *First Aid: Emergency Care for Dogs and Cats* (by Roger W. Gfeller, DVM, and Michael W. Thomas, DVM; with Isaac May). It is available for browsing at www.veterinarypartner.com. You might also want to see if a first-aid training program for pets is offered in your community; call your local animal shelter or humane organization.

Caution

If you have to administer emergency first aid to your dog, as soon as possible thereafter, take her to a veterinarian for follow-up care–even if your dog seems past the crisis. Only a vet can confirm that all is well.

Assemble a first-aid kit. Use a toolbox, a sewing box, or any other container that can conveniently store the following supplies:

- Cotton—roll type and balls
- Gauze pads and tape
- Nonstick bandages
- Scissors
- Muzzle—actual or makeshift, such as strips of cotton, to prevent biting
- Latex gloves
- Towels
- Wet wipes
- Eyewash
- Hydrogen peroxide
- Milk of magnesia

- "Dog stretcher"—large piece of cardboard, exercise mat, or heavy blanket
- Tweezers
- Oral syringes
- Ice pack
- Rectal thermometer

Just as important is what not to include in your kit, and primarily that means drugs. Drug poisoning, reports the American Veterinary Medical Association (AVMA), is the most common cause of poisoning in small animals. You should contact a veterinarian before giving your dog any medication, because even if it is safe in some doses, it may not be safe in human doses. For example, dogs, particularly small dogs, can suffer major tissue damage from as little as two regular-strength acetaminophen tablets (e.g., Tylenol). Dogs are also highly sensitive to the nonsteroidal anti-inflammatory drugs (NSAIDs) found in most pet owners' medicine cabinets—aspirin, ibuprofen (e.g., Advil and Nuprin), and naproxen.

Include other caregivers in your plans. Do you use the services of a pet sitter, a groomer, and/or a dog walker? Give anyone and everyone who comes in regular contact with your dog and is responsible for her care at any time the list of contact numbers you compiled, along with a copy of your dog's medical file. Write down where you can be reached at all times, and supply a secondary local contact name and number for when you will be out of town.

First Aid to Go

First-aid kits for pets come ready-made. One to check out is from Medi+Pet, which contains forty items and a first-aid booklet. Call 888-633-4738, or go online to www.medipet.com. You'll pay for the convenience, though.

Spay/Neuter: Better Late Than Never

Ideally, your dog was spayed or neutered as a youngster. But if not, did you know that doing so is one of the best preventive measures you can take to reduce the risk of serious illness in senior dogs? Many owners of older pets are afraid to submit them to this procedure; but vets agree, it's much less dangerous to have older dogs spayed or neutered than to have them undergo treatment for reproductive organ diseases such as pyometra (females) and prostasis (males), certain cancers, and other diseases more prevalent in "intact" dogs.

Of course, for an older dog, more precautions are necessary, and your veterinarian will have to conduct a thorough exam and run bloodwork and other tests before performing the procedure. But unless your dog is very old or in poor medical condition, spaying or neutering is generally advisable.

Senior-Sensitize Your Home

One of the kindest—and most effective—preventive measures you can take is to adjust your dog's environment, based on her needs. For example:

1. If your dog has arthritis or other joint/muscle problems and your house has stairs, put gates across them, to prevent her from stressing weak and painful joints—or, worse, falling down.
2. If your dog has trouble bending, replace ground-level food and water dishes with elevated versions. Many pet supply stores routinely carry these; or you can purchase them from suppliers such as Doctors Fosters & Smith (www.drsfoster-smith.com) or Senior Pet Products (www.seniorpetproducts.com).
3. If your dog is arthritic, consider using a portable ramp or steps to make her access easier. Both are readily available from Dog Ramp at www.dogramp.com. Likewise, if your dog is

allowed on your bed or other furniture (whose isn't?), give her a step up.

4. Bare floors can be especially problematic for older dogs with mobility problems: they have trouble getting up and down on them and keeping their balance when walking across them. Either cover the areas your dog frequents with nonskid runners or rugs or cover your dog's feet with nonskid "booties" (make your own or check out ready-mades such as those available from www.seniorpetproducts.com). An alternative is to take a tip from show-dog owners, who for years have been spraying their champions' feet with an adhesive-type product, such as Tacky Feet or Show Foot Anti-Slip Spray, to keep them on the mark. (If you choose this option, keep an eye on your dog's feet the first few days, to ensure she doesn't have an allergic reaction to the spray; and leave a sizeable portion unsprayed, as your dog "sweats" through her paws).

5. Similarly, food and water dishes on bare floors cause problems for the older dog: they skid across the floor when the dog's eating. Put a rubber-backed placemat or other nonskid material underneath the bowls to stabilize them. And if your house is large or on several levels, strategically place additional water bowls so that your dog can readily access water at all times (and don't forget to freshen the water at least once a day).

6. Choose your dog's bedding for comfort, not cuteness (although usually you can do both). Many senior dogs with arthritis and other joint ailments do well with so-called eggcrate foam mattresses. You can buy these from one of the pet supply catalogs listed previously, or buy the material yourself from a discount department store such as Wal-Mart or Kmart.

7. If your dog is sensitive to temperature, move her bedding as appropriate to keep her comfortable—for example, away from drafts and windows.

These are just a few suggestions; most people find very creative, innovative, and, often, less expensive (i.e., do-it-yourself) ways to accommodate their dog's needs. And don't give up if one solution doesn't pan out; keep trying: you'll find what works best for you and your dog.

Raise Social Awareness

Like many geriatric humans, older dogs too can become more irritable in general. Hearing or vision loss causes them to be more easily startled or scared, and they may react by growling or snapping. Skin irritations can make them more sensitive to touch—especially unintentionally rough handling from children. Joint and muscle aches make them stubborn and crabby—they don't like to move

Tune In to Pet Care

Dr. Marty Becker, author of the fastest-selling pet book in history, *Chicken Soup for the Pet Lover's Soul*, and veterinary contributor to ABC's *Good Morning America*, is now hosting a weekly radio program, "Top Vets Talk Pets," live at 10:00 a.m. EST on the Health Radio Network. On the one-hour program, Dr. Becker discusses pet health issues and takes listener calls. At the time of this writing, the program, which has the support of the American Animal Hospital Association (AAHA), was being broadcast in just a few U.S. markets, but you can listen in at www.healthradionetwork.com.

from their favorite spots, no matter how inconvenient to their human companions.

If you've had your dog thoroughly checked out and are confident you're doing everything you can to make her as comfortable as possible medically, yet she's still a girl behaving badly, the onus is on you to keep her from getting in trouble. Many older dogs don't like changes in their routine and environment, so you'll need to be vigilant when she's out of her day-to-day element—in particular around strangers, babies, and young children. Keep her on a leash at all times when you take her outside your home—even for the minute it takes to walk down to the mailbox. And if you are bringing home a new baby or a young pet, plan in advance how you intend to introduce your old dog to what she may regard as the "interloper." You might want to call on the services of a behavior counselor to guide you in improving your old dog's social skills. Your vet or local humane organization can recommend a counselor for you. Or go to Association of Companion Animal Behavior Counselors' (ACABC), http://animalbehaviorcounselors.org, and click on "Find a Counselor or Member." Don't wait until the baby's home and in the crib to learn how to help your dog make this important adjustment.

THE STORY OF SMOKIE AND MAX:
OLD DOG MEETS NEW BABY

Smokie, a black seventy-pound Labrador/shepherd mix, came into our lives when she was about eight weeks old. Weighing just seven pounds, we could hold her in one hand. But she grew quickly, and just as quickly became an important member of the family. In her young-adult years, she was prone to allergies in the spring

and fall, but that was her only real health issue, one easily taken care of with an injection of cortisone. I also gave her multivitamins every day.

When Smokie was eight years old, I learned I was pregnant. Having always told friends and family that Smokie was my baby, it was pointed out to me by one and all that

A dog and his boy

that was about to change. All these years Smokie had been the center of attention, and now someone new was coming along to share the spotlight. My husband, Eric, and I were sure Smokie would have no problems adjusting to the new member of our family; but to placate everyone else in our lives, we had a long talk with our vet and read whatever we could find about how to introduce pets to children.

The first thing we did after our son, Max, was born was bring Smokie one of his blankets from the hospital. She immediately claimed it as her own, sniffing it happily and settling onto the couch with it. We did this on a daily basis until it was at last time to introduce them.

I remember carrying Max into the house in his car seat and settling him on the coffee table. Then I called Smokie over. She proceeded to sniff him cautiously, once in a while looking at me as if to ask what "it" was. Then she settled next to me once more, wagging her tail.

For the first few weeks after Max came home, whenever someone came into the house, we made sure they greeted Smokie first. She was never just a dog to us, and we made sure no one forgot that. Luckily, everyone accepted this rule with little complaint.

In the coming months, every time Max cried, Smokie came running. She had to make sure he was all right. And if I didn't hurry over quickly enough to suit her, she would sit next to him, whining until he quieted down.

After several months, I went back to work, and both sets of grandparents took turns watching Max until Eric came home. It quickly became routine in Smokie's world that while Grandma was taking care of Max, it was her time for some one-on-one attention from Grandpa.

Then came the day Max finally took note of the big black nose always pushing at him. He named her "Mum." When he started walking, she began to follow him, always making sure he was safe. If Smokie thought Max was doing something he shouldn't be, or toddling somewhere that might get him into trouble, she would stand in his way and firmly nose him in the opposite direction. If Max persisted, Smokie would bark until she could herd him where she felt it was safe.

Now Max is an active four-year-old and the tables have turned: he bosses Smokie around. They're also terrific playmates: Max will root through Smokie's toy box, showing her all her toys until she picks the one she wants. And Smokie is teaching Max patience: he has learned there are times when she just doesn't want to play, and he understands that.

It was when Smokie turned ten that we started to notice she was slowing down a bit. She wouldn't come upstairs to sleep with us anymore, and even fell partway down the stairs a time or two. A trip to the vet confirmed that she had a slight case of arthritis, so we added glucosamine to her diet. About a year after that, she started nibbling on a couple of "hot spots," and the vet suggested giving her omega-3 fatty acid supplements to help her dry skin. Max enjoys giving Smokie her medicine, and I've found that she takes the capsules from him more willingly than from me. She is very gentle with him; and he is very sweet when he gives them to her, saying, "Come on, Smokie, you have to take your medicine. Good girl."

The depth of their relationship is evident when Max is watching his favorite shows on TV and declares certain characters to be family members and special friends. Smokie is always among those so blessed. She is the Flying Dutchman on *SpongeBob SquarePants*, the whale in *Finding Nemo*, and Rex the dinosaur in *Toy Story*.

What more could an old dog ask?

—*Renee Robertazzi, Queens, New York*

TRUST YOUR INSTINCTS

Access to the most well-educated and best-trained veterinarians, and the most advanced medical technologies and treatments, is for naught without you. Without your intimate knowledge and understanding of your dog, the "best" provider or medication is just something to be bragged about in professional publications and marketing materials. You have to get in touch with that knowledge, and *trust* it. Don't push aside "funny feelings," "gut sensations," or "hunches" when it comes to your dog. Dr. Barbara Kalvig says it's surprising how many pet owners bring in their dogs because "they just have a feeling" something might be wrong—and usually they're right! Often, she says, it's nothing they can even put their finger on—such as one of the signs of aging listed previously—more a vague awareness they feel compelled to follow up on.

What's going on here? Mental telepathy or just one of the many marvelous developments of the canine-human bond, forged thousands of years ago? That's for you to decide; it doesn't really matter whether you attribute such "insider information" to the mystical or the more down to earth. What matters is that you act on it. What have you got to lose: a little time and the cost of a visit to your vet? Small price to pay for peace of mind.

I Hear What You're Saying: Animal Communicators

A growing number of pet owners are calling on the services of animal communicators, who believe it is possible to *exchange* information with animals, most commonly between one person and his or her pet.

Frequent issues raised by clients of animal communicators include: behavior problems, understanding an animal's needs and feelings, working with veterinarians, locating lost animals, learning when an animal is "ready to go," and communicating with a pet after it has died.

If this is an avenue you want to pursue as part of your dog's health care program, be sure to get recommendations for a communicator. Most vets can give you either a direct referral or the name of a client who uses one. And be aware that costs vary widely, from as little as $25/hour to $300/hour.

SUMMARY

An ounce of prevention still is worth a pound of cure—although where an aging dog's health is concerned, that may be an undervaluation. By taking a proactive stance to your dog's health care, you are in the best position to act, and react, conscientiously and with love, no matter what the circumstance. You'll also be better able to read the vital signs your dog may send, which are discussed in the next chapter.

KEY PET POINTS

- You love your dog, of course, but even the most devoted pet owner may, in the course of a busy life, start to take things for granted. Your dog's long-term health depends on your paying attention to the changes she'll be going through as she ages.
- Don't wait until something's wrong to call your vet. Do it now: schedule two appointments, six months apart.
- Expect the best, but plan for the worst. Old dogs are more prone to accidents and sudden illness. Prepare for emergencies: know who you're going to call, where you're going to go, and what to do until you can reach help.
- You're number one in your dog's life, and along with all the unconditional love you enjoy as a result, it also means you know her better than anyone else—including your vet. Trust that knowledge and act on it whenever you think you should.

CHAPTER 3

Vital Signs: Recognizing Signals of Change from Your Dog

Dogs may not be able to express themselves in human language, but they sure can communicate with us. What dog owner doesn't recognize the glad-you're-home bark, or the one that says, "What about me? I'm hungry!" or "Let me in—I've been waiting at the door *forever*." And who doesn't know the whine of suspicion, the red-alert growl, the whimper of fear, or the "I want to go for a walk

now" yap? A dog's body language is just as informative. Rolling on his back in the grass is easily translated as, "This feels great." Sitting practically on top of you and staring intently often means, "Pay attention to me." Blocking the door as you prepare to leave means, "Over my dead body you're going without me." The list is endless. So though dogs don't have a word vocabulary, you could easily compile a dog dictionary of commonly used barks, other vocalizations, and body phrases.

Where dogs have a failure to communicate, however, is when it comes to "describing" physical and mental discomfort. Though they've been domesticated for thousands of years, one instinct they retain from their wilder days is to hide weakness. For as we all know, in nature, "only the strong survive." But this instinct does not serve them well in the human environment, which is tuned to a different frequency, the one that understands and responds to clear, vocal expressions of discomfort. When we humans feel ill, we let someone (or everyone) know about it. Dogs "say" nothing. Fact of the matter is, they may not even be aware of age-related changes taking place unless and until they're in extreme pain, at which point they may yelp or whimper to alert us to their distress. But that's not to say their bodies aren't sending out loud-and-clear early-warning messages to us, their caregivers; they are. It's up to us to change the frequency on our "receptor dials" so we can hear and see those messages and take action to discover what they might mean.

To be sure, more outward signs of aging probably will be readily apparent to you—such as a graying muzzle, increased irritability and decreased energy, altered sleep patterns, a change in eating habits and/or appetite. But some will come on so gradually they might slip by you, or you might be tempted to chalk them up to "old age" and not get them evaluated. But remember what Dr. Goldston said is the most common mistake people make in evaluating the health of their aging dogs: interpreting signs of change as "just getting old," and failing to get them checked out.

That's not to say that your dog has now, or will in the future, the diseases or disorders associated with the changes described here. It does say that these changes associated with the process of aging often are indicators of a developing or existing problem, which, left untreated, can impact your dog's life—and your life with him. That's why I call these "vital" signs—they're fundamental clues to your dog's health, hence his quality of life and life expectancy.

The objective of this chapter is not to alarm you—don't automatically assume your dog has the worst of the associated diseases/disorders/conditions listed in each category (for example, not every lump is a cancer). Nor is it to suggest that you should diagnose your dog based on these signs—in fact, that's the *last* thing you should do.

Rather, the objective is to alert you to common age-related changes so that you can keep track of them and inform your vet at your dog's next checkup, or sooner if the sign is more serious. It's his or her job to determine what—if anything—is wrong and what you can do about it.

BODY PARTS AND FUNCTIONS

This first section breaks down the canine body, and describes how each part might break down, to give you a more thorough understanding of the signs of your dog's physical aging process.

Note

Many of the diseases and disorders associated with age-related changes are covered in Chapter 6.

Metabolism

We humans tend to think of our metabolism primarily as the villain we fight in the battle against weight gain. We envy those people with a "high metabolism," who never seem to gain a pound, and we cite our slowing metabolism as the reason we can't seem to lose weight no matter what we do and what we eat, particularly as we grow older.

Metabolism, both in humans and canines, does slow with aging, so your senior dog is probably starting to gain weight—especially if you've been feeding him essentially the same diet since he was a young adult and if he's getting less exercise than he used to. In serious cases, the result is obesity, which as in the human population has become a major precursor of serious disease in dogs. A decreased metabolic rate, plus lack of activity, reduces caloric need between 30 and 40 percent. That means you probably need to start feeding your dog different food. Details on that are in Chapter 5, "Nutrition, Exercise, and Grooming: Keeping Your Dog in Shape."

Though weight gain is the more typical problem of older dogs, weight loss, too, is an equally important metabolic message, one you'll need your vet to interpret, for metabolism affects more than just how efficiently your dog processes his food. As your dog ages, his immune

---

Obesity: Battle of the Bulge

Obesity is more than a sign, it's a billboard, one that reads in supersize, boldface letters, "Overweight dogs at greater risk." Why then do so many dog owners miss or ignore it? As it turns out, weight, like beauty, seems to be in the eyes of the beholder. According to vets from around the country, many pet owners whose dogs are overweight or obese see their dogs' weight as normal, or correct for their size; furthermore, they often think that an appropriate weight looks too thin.

As a dog owner, in addition to knowing how much your dog weighs, you need to understand what's referred to as "body condition." This gives a much clearer indication of whether your dog needs to lose weight, as it describes how your dog should *look* and *feel* to you. For example, on an ideal-weight dog, you should be able to easily *feel* his ribs through his coat, but not *see* them sticking out. His abdomen should also have a visible "tuck" when viewed from the side.

The Purina Web site (www.purina.com/dogs/nutrition) has easy-to-understand "Body Condition System" descriptions, categorized as Too Thin, Ideal, and Too Heavy, along with drawings. With your dog by your side, take a look at them and compare.

---

competence decreases, and he is less able to ward off infections and is more susceptible to autoimmune diseases.

Signs: weight gain or loss; change in appetite

Associated diseases/disorders/conditions: weight gain—hypothyroidism, Cushing's disease, arthritis; weight loss—kidney, liver, or gastrointestinal disease; oral or dental disease; diabetes mellitus

Muscles, Bones, and Joints

Just like us, as dogs age, they lose muscle, bone, and cartilage mass. The common result: arthritis, greater vulnerability to fractures, and muscle weakness. Even if they don't suffer from arthritis or break a bone, inevitably their joints will stiffen. Overall, your dog will start to be less comfortable and perhaps show signs of weakness or lethargy.

Signs: limping, difficulty getting up and down, sensitivity to cold; greater irritability and less interest in activity

Associated diseases/disorders/conditions: arthritis, hip dysplasia, nervous system dysfunction, obesity

Skin, Hair, and Nails

An older dog's skin thickens, becomes hyperpigmented, and loses elasticity. His footpads may become supersensitive to drying and cracking. His once-glowing coat is now so dry it looks like he's having a bad-hair day every day; or his hair looks greasy and smells the same. His claws grow so fast you can't clip them often enough; and they're brittle as glass and a danger to floors, carpets, and human skin and clothing.

And one day while you're petting him, you suddenly feel a growth—a lump—on or beneath your dog's skin. Lumps and bumps are common to the aging dog. Don't panic: not all are serious, but all should be checked out.

Older dogs are also more sensitive to attack by parasites such as fleas, ticks, worms, and mosquitoes—in some cases, dangerously so.

Roundworm, hookworm, and tapeworm can cause anemia; and heartworm, which is spread by mosquitoes and lodges in the heart, can cause death when left untreated.

Signs: nonstop scratching; dandruff; body odor; hair loss; weird growths or skin discoloration; "hot spots" (sores caused by incessant scratching)

Associated diseases/disorders/conditions: hypothyroidism; Cushing's disease; obesity; parasite invasion; cancer or benign tumors; heartworm

Eyes

Often one of the signs dog owners notice first as a signal of aging is a "cloudy" look to their dog's eyes. Though an obvious alteration, lens cloudiness does not always mean impaired vision; it often is an indication of nuclear sclerosis, which can, however, make it difficult for dogs to see at night or to focus close up.

Of greater concern are two diseases dogs share with humans, glaucoma and cataracts, which can develop simultaneously and can

lead to reduced vision, even blindness. In addition to nuclear sclerosis, the aforementioned whiteness or cloudiness may also be a sign of cataracts, whereas the beginning of glaucoma is signaled by redness—especially sudden onset—or a smaller-than-usual pupil. Dogs can also contract conjunctivitis, an infection that may be prompted by allergies or an abrasion or cut to the eye.

Signs: a white, milky look to the lenses; redness in the whites of the eyes; mucus buildup in the eye and/or discharge; wincing or pawing at the eyes

Associated diseases/disorders/conditions: nuclear sclerosis; cataracts; glaucoma; dry eye; conjunctivitis

Ears

Like people, it's not uncommon for senior dogs to lose their hearing, either partially or entirely. Most dogs generally adapt quite well to this loss; you, on the other hand, may have a harder time of it, as you learn to deal with the frustration of your dog's failure to respond to your verbal commands and calls. Teaching your dog hand signals and relying more on body language can ease the transition. You'll also have to be more careful when your dog is out and about, to protect him from dangers whose only signal is sound—such as that of an oncoming car. Dogs with hearing loss should always be walked on a leash.

In addition, be on the lookout for any unusual discharge from your dog's ears—in particular when it's associated with an unpleasant odor, often signaling an ear infection. Also be aware that as dogs age they become more susceptible to ear mites.

Signs: failure to respond normally to your voice, sounds, other vocal stimuli; incessant scratching around the ears, with accompanying irritation and smelly, excessive discharge

Associated diseases/disorders/conditions: hearing loss/deafness; mites, ear infection

Nose and Throat

Dripping nose, sneezing, and coughing. Sound familiar? Your dog might just have an allergy or a cold. But a cold's nothing to sneeze at in an older dog. A persistent cold could indicate his lungs and bronchial tubes are producing too much mucus, which can lead to much more serious problems (see below). Dogs who have a lot of contact with other dogs (e.g., they go to doggie "day care," frequent dog runs and other common play areas, or are boarded in kennels) are especially susceptible to contagious diseases such as "kennel cough" (infectious tracheobronchitis).

Signs: runny nose; persistent sneezing and coughing; shallow breathing; lack of energy and appetite

Associated diseases/disorders/conditions: cold; bronchitis; kennel cough; pneumonia; heart disease; heartworm; cancer

---

The Nose Knows

Or does it? Yes and no. Many of us were taught that a dry, hot nose was a sure sign our dog was sick and, conversely, that a wet, cool nose was a sign of health. In fact, your dog's nose may change from wet and cool to dry and hot from one minute to the next in the course of the day, based on environment (temperature, humidity, etc.).

That said, a sick dog often will have a hot, dry nose, but the only way to know for sure is to take your dog's temperature, rectally. Other signs from your dog's nose you should follow up on are color change (typically, loss of pigmentation), prolonged dryness and cracking, and any sores or scabs.

Mouth

Do you brush your dog's teeth and gums regularly? If you do, you're in the minority of pet owners, and you're taking one of *the* most important steps to ensuring your dog's long life and good health.

Who's Who in Pet Health Care: American Veterinary Dental College (AVDC)

The AVDC, founded in 1988, is the clinical specialist organization for veterinary dentists. It is accredited by the American Board of Veterinary Specialties of the American Veterinary Medical Association (AVMA). The college is also involved in the prevention of oral disease through its sponsorship of the Veterinary Oral Health Council. Though primarily for professionals, you can learn a lot about companion animal dental care by going to www.avdc.org and clicking on the Pet Owners link.

Many people are surprised to learn that good dental hygiene is one of the most crucial aspects of wellness in dogs. It's about much, much more than bad breath and yellowing teeth. According to one report, 85 percent of dogs (and cats) four years and older suffer from periodontal disease, which left untreated can lead to infection of major organs such as the lungs, kidneys, and liver—even the nervous system—and, eventually, to death. The American Veterinary Dental College (AVDC) says periodontal disease is the most common clinical condition in companion animals. The good news is, periodontal disease is treatable in the early stages.

You'll also want to be on the lookout for any changes to the healthy pink color of your dog's gums, which can signal other problems, such as anemia (pale pink/almost-white gums).

Signs: bad breath; bleeding from the mouth; loose or discolored teeth; trouble eating/chewing; dropping food; drooling; loss of appetite; sensitivity to touch around mouth area; change in gum color

Associated diseases/disorders/conditions: gingivitis; periodontal disease; infection of major organs; oral cancers

THE STORY OF FRISKY:
A TEXTBOOK CASE OF AGING

On a dog-day afternoon in Tucson, Arizona, where there are many such days, the clump of greasy, matted fur didn't know it yet, but his luck was about to change. He was about to be rescued by a woman who had dedicated her life, and inheritance, to saving lost and abandoned dogs in the area.

So unkempt was he that, initially, it was difficult to tell whether he was a cat or a dog. But once bathed and blow-dried, there was no doubt he was all dog—and a damn fine specimen, too: a purebred red Pomeranian.

That was only the beginning of his luck, for his rescuer soon found him a permanent foster home with a retired city employee who loved nothing more in life than dogs. This one won her heart, and she his, on contact.

Dubbed Frisky, he quickly put aside his questionable past and took on an attitude of entitlement, requiring his own way in all things at all times (perhaps he was part cat, after all). How he managed this was through his looks and charm. When in "full bloom," just after a grooming, his thick, fiery-red fur ablaze in the hot southwestern sun, he was a showstopper, especially on prances around the park just across the street from his house. He reveled in the attention, even seeming to grin with pleasure, his pointed nose tilting upward, his mouth open wide in the unmistakable shape of a smile. The look said, "I know I'm cute; everyone tells me that." Children in particular were enchanted by him, often remarking he looked like a little bear.

Guesstimated to be four years old at the time of his rescue, Frisky joined a household with two much older dogs; but within a very short time, they went on to their great reward and Frisky became top dog. He was not alone for long. Soon he was joined by another street rescue, Sammy, a small, white, self-effacing poodle—they were the perfect match. They cohabitated comfortably for years, edging into old age with as much dignity as their foster mother.

But at around age nine or ten, Frisky began to suffer myriad signs of aging. First his teeth started to give him trouble, and no amount of cleaning could save them all; a number had to be pulled. His skin began to torment him, too; it became dry, flaky, and itchy almost beyond relief. Eventually, he had to have his glorious red coat clipped short, to enable easier care of his skin. Then, to add insult to injury, this proud Pomeranian's mind began to go. He wouldn't sleep at night, but sat up staring so intently at his foster mother that he woke her up, too. He seemed confused and lost sometimes: Where *is* the door? Next he began to lose his appetite—and his good manners: if no one let him out immediately when he had to go, he simply couldn't wait.

Frisky's foster mother, though she had a wealth of love to lavish on him, unfortunately did not have a bank account to match. Living on a fixed income, she was unable to afford all of Frisky's dental work, exams and tests, and grooming costs. To his rescue a second time came the woman who had saved him nine years earlier. Never hesitating for a moment, she paid for every exam, test, and treatment Frisky needed.

But at the age of thirteen, Frisky's luck was about to run out. He was diagnosed with chronic renal disease, and interventions failed to make a significant improvement for long. He lived out his days as all senior citizens should, well loved and cared for, and he was allowed to die in his own home, in his own bed.

Heart and Lungs

As it is among the human population, heart failure is a major threat to your dog's health. According to the American Veterinary Medical Association (AVMA), some 3.2 million dogs (of those examined annually in the United States) have some form of *acquired* heart disease (as distinguished from present at birth). Dogs are most prone to two types of heart disease: chronic valvular heart disease and chronic obstructive pulmonary disease (COPD). Unfortunately, early-stage heart disease has few visible signs. Regular checkups are your first line of defense. When diagnosed early, treatments are available. Dogs also suffer from arrhythmias, heartworm disease (which also affects the lungs), and others.

Who's Who in Pet Health Care: American Veterinary Medical Association (AVMA)

The AVMA, a not-for-profit organization founded in 1863, represents more than seventy-two thousand veterinarians working in private and corporate sectors, government, industry, academia, and uniformed services. Its stated mission is to "improve animal and human health and to advance the veterinary medical profession." The AVMA Web site, www.avma.org, is primarily for its members, but public information is available from its Care for Animals and News links.

And speaking of lungs, an aging dog's lungs lose elasticity, and lung secretions become more viscous. The cough reflex decreases, as does the ability to exhale effectively.

Signs: difficulty breathing, even at rest; loss of appetite and weight; intolerance to any exercise, even fainting/collapsing

Associated diseases/disorders/conditions: heart disease/heart failure; heartworm; arrhythmia; pulmonary infection; pulmonary fibrosis

Liver

A dog's liver cells decrease in number as he ages, making the liver less effective in doing what it was designed for: metabolizing food and detoxifying blood. Serious liver-related problems may result unless treated, including forms of cirrhosis, hepatitis, and cancer.

Signs: loss of appetite/weight loss; yellow gums; increased drinking and urination

Associated diseases/disorders/conditions: jaundice; liver failure; internal bleeding

Kidneys and Urinary Tract

The job of the kidneys is to filter toxins and waste products from the blood, by way of the bladder, through urination. When the kidneys fail to function properly, which is very common in aging dogs, they can no longer retain adequate amounts of water to get the job done. The result is kidney disease, which unfortunately may not show signs until it is well established.

Because the kidneys are part of the urinary tract, urinary tract infections (UTIs) have some of the same symptoms as kidney disease. But UTIs are much easier to treat—usually with a regimen of antibiotics. Your vet will have to run blood tests and require urine specimens to determine which it is.

Other common urinary system disorders of the geriatric dog are incontinence (which can result from a UTI), bladder tumors (the most common tumor of the urinary tract); and, in male dogs, prostatic disorders.

Signs: increased, sometimes insatiable, thirst; frequent need to urinate (though in the case of a UTI, with very little urine as a result); incontinence; blood in urine; loss of appetite

Associated diseases/disorders/conditions: chronic renal failure; urinary tract infection; enlarged prostate (in male dogs); bladder tumor

Tricky Diagnosis

Other diseases may mimic the signs of kidney disease, including liver disease, diabetes, and Cushing's disease. Only your vet can make a conclusive diagnosis, by conducting blood and urine tests and, possibly, taking X-rays and ultrasounds of the kidneys.

Digestive and Elimination Systems

A senior dog's digestive system can seem a study in contrasts. One dog may lose all interest in eating (perhaps because of a diminished sense of smell and taste) and start to lose weight, while another may seem interested in nothing but eating, and begin packing on the pounds. Either way, chances are neither is getting the nutrition he needs from his food, because the aging dog's digestive system loses the ability to absorb nutrients. Proper nutrition, a vital factor in maintaining your dog's health, is covered in Chapter 5, "Nutrition, Exercise, and Grooming: Keeping Your Dog in Shape." For now, recognize that your dog's interest—or lack thereof—in food may be a sign of other problems, so always bring changes in appetite and weight to the attention of your vet.

As your dog ages, he may have trouble keeping his food down. Vomiting occasionally is not uncommon, and usually is a sign of nothing more serious than an upset stomach or that it's time to

Dog Watch Reminder List

- **Respiration:** Note unusual panting (unrelated to exercise) and prolonged coughing and sneezing.

- **Mobility:** Note any difficulty climbing stairs, getting in and out of the car, or rising from and lowering to a resting position; limping or any change in gait; loss of balance or sudden collapses.

- **Coat and skin:** Watch for lumps and bumps; monitor any sores for healing; note hair loss and changes to skin color and texture; keep nails clipped, and note changes or sensitivity to footpads.

- **Food and water:** Note both increased/decreased food/water consumption. Also note any new preferences—for canned food over dry, for example. Watch for signs of difficulty chewing and/or swallowing.

- **Weight:** Gains or losses can be gradual, so it's a good idea to weigh your dog on a regular basis—say, every two months. Any sudden and dramatic changes should, of course, be brought to the attention of your vet.

- **Elimination:** Monitor changes in color, consistency, and amount. Keep an eye out for blood in both stool and urine and for signs of pain while urinating/defecating. Note, too, lapses in housebreaking.

- **Behavior:** Tune into personality changes, such as increased irritability or anxiety; also watch for differences in sleep pattern and other patterns of behavior (such as ignoring voice commands, or failure to greet you at the door).

change his diet to one more tolerable to his more sensitive digestive system. But persistent vomiting is grave cause for concern, especially if there's blood or other foreign material in it. Likewise, retching—the action of vomiting, but with nothing to show for it—is serious business.

You may notice a similar set of contrasts in your dog's elimination system: he may have diarrhea or constipation, or he may suffer both from time to time. When either is short-lived, it's probably nothing to worry about; but if your dog regularly suffers from one or both, or for more than a day or two, it's time to check with your vet. In the case of diarrhea, your dog can quickly become dehydrated, a serious condition; and prolonged constipation can be the sign of an intestinal blockage or tumor. (Note: Urination was covered above, under "Kidneys and Urinary Tract.")

Signs: overeating/undereating; vomiting or retching; diarrhea or constipation

Associated diseases/disorders/conditions: gastrointestinal disease; inflammatory bowel disease; kidney or liver disease; diabetes; cancer; reaction to medications

Tough Duty

It's not the most pleasant task in the world, to be sure, but it's an important one when it comes to caring for your aging dog: paying attention on a regular basis to the color and consistency of your dog's stool. This will be easier for urban dog owners, who walk their dogs and who must abide by pooper-scooper laws; suburban and rural dog owners whose pets run free in a yard or on open land will have to make a more concerted effort. In any case, at some point, your vet will ask you to provide a stool sample as part of your dog's wellness workup.

BRAINS AND BEHAVIOR

Have you been wondering lately whether your dog's mind—you should excuse the expression—is "going to the dogs" these days? Has his behavior changed dramatically, and in a very short period of time? Does he fail to recognize you or others in your household? Does he seem lost or confused in his own home or other familiar surroundings? Does he pace or sit up all night instead of sleeping? Does he bark ceaselessly, at nothing? Is your formerly accident-free good boy now breaking all house rules and using the living room carpet as his private bathroom?

Chances are your dog has lapsed into senility. To be more specific, he may be suffering from cognitive dysfunction syndrome (CDS) (a.k.a. "doggie Alzheimer's"). Only a thorough workup by your vet can determine this, but you'll want to find out as soon as possible because, as in humans, there is no cure, but there are ways to slow down the progression of this disease.

Signs: barking/whining for no apparent reason; sleeplessness; pacing; confusion/disorientation; failure to recognize family; uncharacteristic aggressiveness and/or anxiety; loss of house-breaking

Associated diseases/disorders/conditions: senility; cognitive dysfunction syndrome (CDS)

SUMMARY

If it seems there's a lot to absorb in this chapter, keep in mind you don't have to remember all the details, just the concept of awareness, of tuning into signals your dog may be sending you. In the future, you'll be surprised how much you recall when, say, your dog has a bout of diarrhea, suddenly loses his appetite, or develops an insatiable thirst. You may not remember what those signs mean exactly, but you will know you need to address them. And that's everything. Well, not quite, but it's a great start to everything you can do to take proper care of your aging dog.

KEY PET POINTS

- Keep track of signals from your dog that he is undergoing age-related changes. (Use the checklist in Chapter 2 as a starting point, and add to it as necessary so that you can present it to your vet at your dog's next checkup.)
- Never assume any changes you notice are just "due to getting old," and ignore them.
- Inform yourself as to the problems that may be associated with your dog's physical and behavioral changes, but never self-diagnose based on this information.

PART 2

Geriatric Canine Health Care

CHAPTER 4

Wellness Programs: Keeping Your Dog Healthy for the Long Term

Traditionally, health care was for the sick. Doctors were consulted only when something was wrong. Later, the concept of preventive medicine emerged, with the realization that many illnesses and diseases could be forestalled or more effectively managed by taking proper precautions. Preventive measures were also seen as a way to reduce health care costs, for clients, practitioners, and insurance com-

panies alike. But the focus was still on sickness and disease. Today, the approach to health care is distinctly positive: the focus is on *wellness*, and maintaining it for as long as possible.

A skeptic, of course, might regard the term "wellness program" as just the latest in health care jargon, rather than as a legitimate way to improve the way health care is practiced in this country. But even if using the word "wellness" serves the purpose of changing our attitude, might it not be valuable for that reason alone? Isn't it better to think "healthy" instead of "sick," and direct our attention to staying well for as long as possible?

That's certainly the objective of veterinary wellness programs, which are now almost universally being implemented in veterinary practices and hospitals across the country. Gone are the days when vets expected to see pets only in emergencies and for such things as law-mandated vaccinations or flea and tick control. Today, vets recommend that all pets receive an annual checkup and, beginning at age seven, a biannual—twice yearly—exam.

What Bugs Dogs Most?

According to the State of the American Pet Survey (commissioned by the Healthy Pets 21 Consortium of the Purina Pet Institute), the three most common health problems of dogs of all ages are: fleas and ticks, ear infections, and allergies.

In no category of pet care is the concept of wellness more important than the geriatric age group. Says Dr. Richard Goldston, "It has been repeatedly documented that many of the chronic disorders and disease processes seen in geriatric pets can be either cured or at least medically controlled if they are detected early enough." That's why this chapter is devoted in large part to explaining what's involved in standard wellness exams, which can be broadly divided into two categories:

• Exams for healthy-appearing dogs
• Exams for sick or unhealthy dogs

But before you can take your dog for her wellness exam, you must have a veterinarian. Many of you already have one—ideally someone who has been working with you and your dog since your first days together, and is very familiar with your dog's history and health status. If so, you can skip the next section for now; refer to it later if you need to (for example, if you need a second opinion at

National Pet Wellness Month: Helping Vets Help Pets

In 2004, the American Veterinary Medical Association (AVMA) teamed with Fort Dodge Animal Health, a manufacturer and distributor of animal health care products, to launch National Pet Wellness Month (NPWM), a two-pronged year-round initiative designed to: (1) educate pet-owners about the importance of biannual wellness exams and, (2) to aid veterinarians in implementing wellness programs into their practices and improving practitioner–pet owner communications.

The level of support in the veterinary community was evident in the turnout for the inaugural campaign, held in October 2004: more than 10,000 veterinary clinics, comprising some 40 percent of all clinics in the United States, signed up.

For more on this campaign and consumer information on veterinary wellness programs, visit either www.npwm.com or www.avma.org.

---

some point down the road). But you might not already have a vet. If that's the case, don't wait to begin your search for one—this must be the first step in any senior dog wellness program.

Starting Now

It's never too late to begin a wellness program for your dog. Even if you've been lucky and your dog has had no health problems so far, if you haven't been taking her to see a vet regularly, now is the best time to start—for both of you. Beginning a regular care program now, no matter how old your dog, will pay off in the future, either by preventing costly problems later or making it possible to manage health care concerns more effectively.

FINDING A VET

What's the best way to find a vet who interacts well with you and your dog and provides quality care? First, you need to identify your "search criteria," which may include:

- Location
- Hours of service
- Range of services. For example, can surgery be performed at the office, or would you have to take your dog to another location?
- Type of practice. Is it a traditional, holistic, or integrative (combines traditional with holistic/alternative) practice?
- Hospital and professional affiliations. Is the doctor a member of the AVMA, for example?
- Emergency care handling. Is a twenty-four-hour on-call service provided?
- Fee/payment structure
- Personal approach. Do you feel comfortable with the behavior of the vet, technicians, office staff, and anyone else who will come in contact with your and your pet?
- Ability to communicate. Does the vet explain things clearly and in lay terms, so that you can understand your pet's condition and what's expected of you? Will the vet or someone on staff be available to train you if you need help medicating or treating your dog—from giving a pill (which is never as easy at home as it looks in the vet's office) to administering injections to a dog with diabetes?

After you've identified your criteria, you might want to take the additional step of prioritizing them. For example, if you're on a tight budget, fee/payment structure may take precedence over location. Or, to you, the most important criterion may be to work with someone who is willing to consider alternative treatment options before, or in conjunction with, prescription medications. Obviously, your choices could be limited, or virtually unlimited, depending on where you live. Big-city dwellers can pick and choose among

Vet-to-Pet Service

D octors making house calls to see their human patients has long been a thing of the past. Our pets are more fortunate. In many areas of the country, they can get vet-to-pet service, which you may want to consider for a number of reasons:

- Perhaps your pet freaks out in the vet's office (a very common trauma). In her own home, where she is more secure, more herself, the vet can more easily evaluate her condition—especially her behavior.
- If your dog is very old and has a compromised immune system for any reason, you reduce the risk of her being exposed to the infections of other sick animals by having her examined at home.
- Your dog may be at the end of her life and you're providing hospice care, with the help of your vet (more on this in Chapter 9).
- You have more than one animal, and rather than having to take them in one at a time, the house-call vet can do a "group" exam.
- Maybe you have no transportation, or you, yourself, are incapacitated for some reason, but your pet needs care.

If you already have a vet, he or she may provide this service, if not generally then in special circumstances, such as for a very old or sick dog. Otherwise, to find a vet who makes house calls in your area, contact the American Association of Housecall Veterinarians (AAHV) at www.athomevet.org.

numerous vets, whereas rural dwellers may have access to only one practice within a twenty-five-mile (or more) radius.

Generally, pet owners find their veterinarians in one of three ways:

Recommendation. This is far and away the preferred way to go. Ask a friend, family member, or other dog owner (dog lovers have a bond, even when they don't know each other well). Just remember, though: a vet that's right for one person and dog may not be right for you and yours. As in all things involved in your pet's care, trust your instincts and do your homework.

Breed clubs. If yours is a purebred dog, these organizations may be the place to go for referrals to qualified vets. Start with the American Kennel Club Web site, www.akc.org, for club information.

Veterinary directories. Whether online or through the Yellow Pages, if you choose this option, it's a good idea to choose at least three names and "vet" them all, as described below.

I Swear . . .

In November 1999, the American Veterinary Medical Association (AVMA) adopted the following practitioner's oath:

Being admitted to the profession of veterinary medicine, I solemnly swear to use my scientific knowledge and skills for the benefit of society through the protection of animal health, the relief of animal suffering, the conservation of animal resources, the promotion of public health, and the advancement of medical knowledge.

I will practice my profession conscientiously, with dignity, and in keeping with the principles of veterinary medical ethics.

I accept as a lifelong obligation the continual improvement of my professional knowledge and competence.

Once you have the name of a vet, schedule an appointment to meet with him or her. You might want to consider going dog-less to this first meeting, so that you can really focus on how the office is run, evaluate whether it's clean and orderly (give it the sniff test, too), and watch how other animals and their owners are treated. Ask for a tour of the facilities (keeping in mind that some rooms may be off-limits due to ongoing treatment or surgery). No conscientious vet will refuse this request; if he or she does, keep looking. Ask for a copy of the practice's policies and procedures. (Note: You'll probably have to pay for this interview.)

Who Ya Gonna Call?

Pet owners turn most often to veterinarians for information about their pets (78 percent according to the Purina's State of the American Pet Survey, and 98 percent according to the AAHA's 2004 Pet Owner Survey).

If the vet passes the people test, schedule an appointment for your dog's first checkup, and base your final decision on how that is conducted. (You'll have a good basis for comparison after reading the rest of this chapter.)

One final important point here: though the caseload of many—maybe most—veterinarians in this country today is made up of a high percentage of senior and geriatric animals, that is not to say that all vets are equally capable of handling the numerous problems presented by this population. If, for whatever reason, you feel that your dog is not getting the proper care (again, trust your instincts), waste no time in seeking a second opinion, consulting a veterinary specialist, or finding a new primary caregiver who is better equipped to give her—and you—the care you both need and deserve.

THE STORY OF MARCELLO: WHERE THERE'S A WILL THERE'S A WAY

Marcello, a black standard poodle, was the one in a litter of ten that knew how to stand out in a crowd. Though his soon-to-be owner had always previously had female dogs, this pup—the "biggest and baddest, yet sweet" male—quickly endeared himself to her.

Though willful, he was not an alpha male; in addition to his two human companions, Audrey and Joseph, he lived with his birth mother, and in all things deferred to her. It was his nature to "run with the pack." It was also his nature to climb—"like a mountain goat, over everything," says Audrey. No box was big enough, no stairs steep enough: if Marcello wanted to go somewhere, he found a way—up, over, and out.

Marcello; Willful and wonderful

When his mother died when he was around five, Marcello became even more bonded to his human parents—in particular, Joseph, whom he accompanied to work every day. For several years, Marcello lived a happy, healthy life, never needing anything beyond basic care from his vet.

But, eventually, his exuberance and penchant for climbing got him into trouble. Already at risk for bone and joint problems due to his breed and size, Marcello's determination to get where he wanted to go elevated the risk. And he lived in a duplex, which meant going up and down stairs was just part of daily life for him. When he was around eleven, Marcello was injured.

Fortunately for him, his owners were as strong willed as he was. Though they were certain Marcello had dislocated a shoulder, the vet they had been taking him to for years was unable to do anything for the dog. Remembers Joseph, "The first time something was wrong, he couldn't help." Convinced Marcello could be helped, Audrey and Joseph wasted no time in seeking the advice of a specialist. Initially, because of Marcello's age, however, the specialist was reluctant to perform shoulder replacement surgery. But, Audrey says, "We knew Marcello had the heart to will himself to recover," and so they went ahead with the surgery.

She was right. They prevailed and so did he—though he made it challenging for them. After the surgery, Audrey and Joseph tried to set up Marcello downstairs, but he would have none of it; no matter what they did to keep him down, he always found a way to make it up.

But in the two years following the surgery, in spite of Herculean efforts by Audrey and Joseph, Marcello began to suffer more mobility problems, including hip dysplasia and arthritis, as well as a neurological defect. For a time these were managed, variously, with prescription medications such as Rimadyl, holistic remedies, and acupuncture. Joseph and Audrey even custom-crafted booties for him, out of balloons (because the store-bought styles didn't fit), to give him traction for standing up and lying down. "Everything worked for a while," says Joseph, "then lost effectiveness."

Then Marcello broke his other shoulder, and began retaining his stool and urine (even when Joseph carried him to his favorite tree). But "his appetite and his spirit were still intact," remembers Audrey, making their decision to let him go just shy of his fourteenth birthday the most difficult of their lives.

THE WELLNESS EXAM

Whether your senior dog appears healthy, is experiencing signs of illness, or has a preexisting disease or disorder, the standard wellness exam will have these elements:

- History
- Complete physical exam
- Screening tests
- Diet and exercise considerations
- Behavior evaluation
- Pharmacological considerations
- Immunizations (vaccinations)

The exact composition of tests and considerations will, however, be based on your dog's age and health status at the time of the exam.

To compile a comprehensive history on your dog's health, your vet will probably ask you both yes/no-type questions and more open-ended questions in a number of categories. He or she may also ask you to fill out a printed historical record, similar to those you fill out prior to your own physical exam. So come prepared to answer questions covering these topics:

- Medications (including prescription, over-the-counter, vitamins, and herbs)
- Previous surgeries or other procedures
- Behavioral changes
- Physical changes
- Appetite
- Level of activity/exercise
- Quality of life

Questions in these categories will apply whether your dog appears healthy, is showing signs of disease/dysfunction, or has already been diagnosed with one or more diseases/disorders.

Share the Wellness

t's official: pets are good for our health. So say the scientists who study such things, and in increasing numbers.

As if we didn't already know. Anyone who has had their dog nuzzle and lick their cares away knows that the best medicine comes not in capsule form, but in fur form. But in no demographic are the pet-to-people benefits so dramatic as in the human senior citizen category.

THE FACTS

Consider these priceless advantages for seniors living with a pet, as reported by the Pet Food Institute:

- A study of Medicare recipients reported that seniors sharing their lives with dogs had 21 percent fewer visits to the doctor.
- A study of heart patients revealed that people who owned pets had lower blood pressure and cholesterol levels.
- Seniors with pets report fewer incidences of depression and are less lonely.

That's not all: seniors with pets exercise more; they are more active socially; and in the process of taking care of their dogs, they take better care of themselves.

According to the *International Journal of Aging and Human Development*, many Americans would rather live in a place that allowed pets than in a more convenient place that doesn't. Fortunately, today all states now allow pets in nursing homes. (Did you know it's against the law for federally assisted senior facilities to discriminate against pet owners? Pass it on.) And the *Journal of the American Geriatrics Society* reported, in May 1999, that seniors living alone with pets tend to have better physical health and a sense of well-being than those without a furry friend.

Even those senior citizens who don't have their own pets can benefit by visits from them. Hospitals and nursing homes that support "pet therapy" programs report patients are more receptive to treatment, have greater incentive to recover, and a stronger will to live. That's as good as it gets.

SENIOR-PET MATCHUP PROGRAMS

In recognition of the good that pets can do for senior citizens, and vice versa, a number of programs have been developed to encourage these relationships. Here are two:

- *Pets for the Elderly Foundation (PEF).* This nonprofit organization "provides the gift of health and happiness to senior citizens in need" by making donations to animal shelters across America for the purpose of providing the elderly with a companion pet at no charge (including adoption fee, spay/neuter fee, immunizations, and follow-up visits). Approximately fifty-five shelters nationwide participate in the program, which has saved nearly five thousand pets—and, of course, brought joy into the lives of many seniors. (For more on The PEF, go to www.petsfortheelderly.org, or call 866-849-3598, toll free.)

- *Partnering Animals with Seniors (P.A.W.S.).* Launched by the Arizona Humane Society (AHS), P.A.W.S. is for people sixty or older who want to share their lives with a pet. According to AHS Online, the focus of P.A.W.S. is to find homes for older companion animals in its care—a classic senior matchup. (For more on P.A.W.S., go to www.azhumane.org.)

To find out if such a program exists in your community, contact your local humane organization; or the headquarters of the Humane Society of the United States (HSUS) at 202-452-1100 or www.hsus.org; or the American Society for the Prevention of Cruelty to Animals (ASPCA) at 212-876-7700 or www.aspca.org.

Coming to Terms

You may have noticed the use here of the terms "healthy-appearing" and "apparently healthy." It's not hedging. Vets use these phrases for clarity and precision. Recall that your dog, which may seem perfectly healthy to you, may in fact have "subclinical" indications of a problem, meaning she is showing no signs that she can feel or that you can see.

However, if your dog has already been diagnosed, the "history questions" will be expanded to cover response to/compliance with treatment (therapies, medication, etc.), adherence to/acceptance of dietary changes, and others, depending on your dog's specific condition. And if your dog is seriously ill, you'll be asked more in-depth questions about quality of life, so that your vet can better manage pain and other effects of the disease, and treatments, as appropriate.

History

The first stage of the wellness exam is, essentially, a background check—your dog's history. If this is your dog's first visit, expect it to be more comprehensive than if you have a prior relationship with the vet and he or she already has your dog's *baseline data*—the initial set of observations to use for future comparison.

Physical Exam

Your dog's physical exam starts even before the hands-on process begins. The vet does a visual overview—to evaluate posture, quality of gait, signs of stress or discomfort, quality of gaze and coat, and so on. Then the complete physical begins, from "nose to toes," as Dr. Goldston calls it. The *apparently healthy senior dog's* physical will include, but not be limited to, the following, based on her age and history:

Vital signs: temperature, pulse, and respiration (TPR)

Weight: gain or loss, obesity, marked changes in appetite

Musculoskeletal evaluation: mobility, muscle mass, gait, joint "cracking," weakness and/or pain

Cardiopulmonary evaluation (heart and lungs): heart rate and rhythm, pulse rate and quality

"Outer" dog: quality of skin, coat, and claws, and nail bed characteristics

Central nervous system: mental activity, nerve reflexes

Eyes and ears: signs of deterioration, infection, or disease

Abdominal: palpation to determine size and shape of kidneys and liver

Other: risk factor analysis, hydration, rectal palpation, signs of lymph node enlargement

Mouth: signs of gum or dental disease, quality of care

For the senior dog experiencing signs of disease or disorder, the physical exam will be more extensive. It will include a detailed evaluation of any organs showing signs of disease or dysfunction. Your dog will also be carefully monitored for indications of cognitive dysfunction syndrome (CDS)—"doggie Alzheimer's"—such as disorientation, sleep disturbances, confusion, increased anxiety, and loss of housebreaking. The diagnosis aspect will focus on these common senior dog problems:

- Arthritis
- Cancers
- Gastrointestinal disorders
- Weight changes
- Cardiac disease
- Renal disease
- Diabetes
- Hypothyroidism
- Respiratory disorders

The symptoms and changes you have reported to your vet since your last visit, along with the vet's own observations during this check-up, will determine any future testing in these areas (see Chapter 6).

And for the *seriously ill senior dog*, an important focus of the exam will be on pain management, quality of life, and, potentially, hospice care, all of which you'll learn more about later in the book. Behavior problems will be major considerations, too, as these become more apparent with increased loss of mobility, pain, and/or anxiety.

Taking TPR

Ask your vet what your dog's normal temperature and pulse and heart rate should be. You might also consider learning how to take these vital signs. Knowing how to do this will better enable you to determine when something is wrong at home. Your vet can show you the proper way to take these measurements.

Screening Tests

This is often the most challenging aspect of the wellness exam for dog owners, for most of it takes place out of your sight. Although you probably will be present when, for example, your dog's blood is drawn, the actual screening of the blood will be done in a lab by a technician doing procedures you wouldn't understand even if you could be present. What's more, the language of medical testing is unintelligible to most pet owners, unless they happen to work in the medical profession, too.

That said, it's still a good idea to familiarize yourself with the common screening tests your dog will undergo as part of her wellness exam. For a *healthy-appearing senior dog*, these include:

- Complete blood count
- Complete urinalysis
- Internal parasite exam (for heartworm and internal parasites)
- Fecal analysis
- Total calcium and protein
- Additional tests, as necessary based on age, breed, sex, medical history, and current medications

For the *senior dog experiencing signs of disease or disorder*, expect the screening tests to include those listed above, plus:

- Confirmatory tests
- Biopsies, if necessary
- As required: X-rays, ultrasound, echocardiography, and contrast studies
- Potentially others, based on condition

Learn Your ABCs

If you've ever watched hospital shows on television, you've no doubt been stupefied by the shorthand doctors use to refer to various tests and procedures. Vets are no different. To help you navigate the alphabet soup, here are some of the most common abbreviations you may hear in the vet's office or see on invoices or other paperwork:

- BCP: blood chemistry profiles
- CBC: complete blood count
- CDS: cognitive dysfunction syndrome
- DA2PPV: distemper/adenovirus/parvovirus/parinfluenza
- OCD: obsessive compulsive disorder
- TSH: thyroid stimulating hormone
- UA: urinalysis

Any others you hear and don't understand, ask.

Nutrition and Exercise

The findings of the physical exam and the screening test components of the wellness program will enable your vet to develop a nutritional plan that's right for your aging dog. According to Dr. Goldston:

Many new diets have been precisely formulated for older pets having high-risk factors for certain diseases, or for those having early degenerative aging changes in various organ systems. Choosing and feeding a diet scientifically formulated for a specific organ disorder, such as kidney failure, heart disease, liver or pancreatic insufficiency, digestive disorders, and so on, will slow down the degenerative processes and either improve the organ function or, in some cases, reduce the workload of the organ. This will improve how your pet feels and may prolong its life. It's a win–win situation for you and your pet.

Based on the results of those two exam components, your vet may recommend, for example:

- Increasing your dog's protein intake (*unless* your dog has been diagnosed with renal disease).
- Switching to one of the stage-of-life diets—for example, premium "senior" or "less active" brands, if you buy her food from a grocery store or pet supply store; or to a "prescription" dog food, which is available for purchase only from veterinary offices.
- Adding an antioxidant to your dog's diet.
- Starting an exercise program.

And if your dog is overweight or obese, your vet no doubt will recommend a weight reduction program; or in the case of a diagnosed disease, a therapeutic diet to help manage it. Finally, you'll be asked to begin to carefully monitor your dog's consumption of both water and food.

These two components of your dog's health program are covered more fully in the next chapter, "Nutrition, Exercise, and Grooming: Keeping Your Dog in Shape."

Medications, Herbs, and Supplements

As with nutrition and diet, this segment of the exam is entirely dependent on the findings of the complete physical and screening tests. And any remedies chosen will depend in part on whether you take your dog to a veterinarian who practices traditional, holistic, or integrative medicine or if you work with more than one type of practitioner. Chapter 6 will give you more information on these topics.

Vaccinations

Probably you're most familiar with this aspect of your dog's health care. It may be the first reason you took your dog to the vet, to vaccinate her as required by law and to protect her against infectious diseases such as rabies. Vaccines trigger protective immune responses; some can reduce the severity of future diseases while others can prevent infection altogether.

Veterinarians categorize vaccinations as "core" and "noncore." Core vaccines (which include rabies, distemper, parvovirus, and hepatitis) are recommended for most pets; noncore vaccines are given based on the specific needs of the pet, geographic location, and discretion of the doctor. Common noncore vaccines include those to protect against Lyme disease and leptospirosis (viral or bacterial infections).

For years, vaccinations were given routinely every year. More recently, however, it has been discovered that some vaccines provide immunity that lasts much longer than a year, while others offer protection for less than a year. Moreover, it has been found that some dogs that get yearly shots develop tumors, called sarcoma, at the immunization site. Both these issues raise the question of the wisdom of vaccinating an older dog—particularly a much older dog. Fortunately, today the standard practice is to design customized vaccination programs for each pet, taking into consideration factors such as age, health, and environment (certain diseases, such as Lyme, are more prevalent in certain parts of the country than others). Lifestyle, too, is taken into account: if your dog rarely goes out, and comes into contact with other dogs only infrequently, she is probably at less risk of exposure to infectious disease. Dr. Goldston reports that:

> For more than five years now, I have been limiting vaccines to the pediatric series of core vaccines, followed by vaccinations every three years, instead of annually on the core vaccines. I still believe all adult pets should be seen yearly and subsequently I give the canine distemper vaccine one year, the canine parvovirus vaccine the next year, and the

rabies vaccine the third year, and just keep that going until the geriatric years, when they are vaccinated on the basis of benefit-versus-risk assessment by me and the owner.

Also, I use the benefit-versus-risk assessment on many adult pets. Examples include not vaccinating any [dogs] after four or five years that are rarely exposed, such as pets that are not routinely boarded.

But, Goldston points out, sometimes the law and politics interfere with best veterinary practices. He says that most counties and many states have rabies vaccination laws that mandate overvaccination. Sometimes this is done less for health reasons than for money reasons—rabies license fees often pay for the county animal control department.

To help customize your dog's vaccination program, some vets may recommend tests called *serologic titers*, which theoretically measure antibody response. "Theoretically" is the operative word here, for these tests are not considered reliable, says the AVMA, because there is no way to ascertain "that a specific concentration of antibody is always protective or that a lower concentration leaves an animal unprotected." If your vet wants to take this test, don't hesitate to ask for an explanation.

Lurking in the Shadows

Thanks to vaccines, from time to time throughout history certain widespread infectious diseases have become so uncommon that they were believed to be eradicated and that vaccinations were no longer necessary. In fact, though, the disease agents continue to be present in the environment, lying in wait for the right opportunity and host, to reemerge as deadly as ever.

THE YOU FACTOR

There's one other component of the wellness exam, and it has everything to do with you: it's the point during the exam when your veterinarian *educates* you—whether it's to emphasize the importance of brushing your dog's teeth; to inform you about the signs of change to watch for in your dog between this visit and the next; or to advise you how to keep your old dog mentally stimulated if she's beginning to show the signs of "doggy Alzheimer's." At a minimum, look for your vet to review with you:

- The common diseases/syndromes of older dogs and your role in helping to detect them
- The importance of compliance in giving medications exactly as prescribed
- The importance of controlling weight—monitoring either for gain or loss—and sticking to an exercise regimen (including mental stimulation)
- The significance of keeping a log of your dog's progress and changes
- Environmental adjustments you may need to make to accommodate disability or weakness and to maintain quality of life
- If necessary, the benefit of spaying/neutering

SUMMARY

The legendary actress Bette Davis said, "Getting old is not for sissies!" She was right, of course. Well, caring for an aging loved one is not for sissies, either. But when you take your dog for biannual wellness exams, you give yourself a leg up on the process: you know where she stands, healthwise; you partner with your vet, so you know you have support at all times; and you prepare yourself for your responsibilities. The reward, of course, is more and better-quality time with your dear dog.

It won't be easy a lot of the time. And in the next chapter, we take on three aspects of senior dog care that many pet owners find the most challenging: nutrition, exercise, and grooming.

KEY PET POINTS

- The best start to giving your aging dog the care she needs is to put yourself in a "wellness" mind-set.
- Interview your vet as you would any professional person providing you with a service. Take into account both your needs and the needs of your aging dog. Do not hesitate to seek second opinions, consult with veterinary specialists, or to switch to a new primary vet.
- Prepare yourself for the extensive nature of the standard geriatric wellness exam. Whether your dog appears healthy or already has some age-related health issues, she will receive a comprehensive physical exam and standard tests, plus other evaluations depending on her age and condition.
- Clarify what you will be required to do in carrying out the recommendations of your dog's vet following the wellness exam.

CHAPTER 5

Nutrition, Exercise, and Grooming: Keeping Your Dog in Shape

Nearly every day it seems we hear or read something about the importance of proper nutrition and adequate exercise to maintaining our health. It's no different for our dogs. So you will already be familiar with many of the concepts presented in this

chapter. That's the good news. The bad news is, many pet owners have as much difficulty implementing effective diet and exercise programs for their dogs as they do for themselves. Therefore, in addition to explaining the specific effects of diet and exercise on aging dogs, a primary objective here is to convince you of the importance of incorporat-

ing regimens for both in your dog's health care program.

As to the third topic of this chapter, grooming, you're very familiar with it, too—though we humans are primarily concerned with it for reasons having to do with how we look and present ourselves to others, personally and professionally. Dogs don't care what they look like (although anyone who has seen a just-groomed dog showing off might understandably dispute that). For dogs, grooming is a health issue, pure and simple, and for senior dogs, it can be a major

Dangerous Diets

A poor or inappropriate diet may contribute to:

- Obesity, from overfeeding, especially foods high in fat and calories
- Diabetes, from food toxins
- Allergies or food intolerance, from chemical preservatives and poor-quality ingredients
- Heart disease and hypertension, from high-sodium foods
- Some cancers, from chemical preservatives

Dr. Goldston says the most common cause of disease/ailment in aging dogs that we *can control* is overfeeding. He cites research done by Purina over the course of fifteen years that showed dogs live two years longer and develop chronic disease such as diabetes and arthritis two years later when they are fed a restricted amount of food, as compared to dogs that were not fed restricted amounts of the same food.

---

one. Older dogs that are not groomed properly and on a regular basis are more susceptible to a whole range of problems, which you'll learn about later in the chapter.

THE PATH TO GOOD NUTRITION

Ideally, you have already made the first step on the path to good nutrition for your senior dog by taking him for his first of two wellness exams this year. And based on the findings of the physical exam and the screening tests conducted, your vet should have given you what Dr. Goldston calls a "nutritional consultation." (If your vet did not, ask for it.)

Remember, the metabolism of older dogs slows, usually making it necessary to reduce their caloric intake accordingly. Even if your

Obesity: It's Not Just for People Anymore

One in four dogs is overweight or obese, according to the National Academy of Science, making it the most common nutritional problem in pets today. Though still lagging behind the 50 percent of the human population estimated to be obese, dogs are catching up—with an accompanying rise in associated health problems—among them diabetes, heart problems, arthritis, hip dysplasia, and endocrine diseases—and a shortened lifespan. Aggravating the risk is that excess weight makes it more difficult for veterinarians to do their job.

Top factors contributing to obesity are: age, spay/neuter status, type of diet, "free" and treat feeding, portion size, and level of exercise. The first factor, obviously, you can do nothing about. The benefits of the second, spaying/neutering your dog, outweigh its implication in weight gain. But the others you can do something about. If your dog is obese, ask yourself:

- Have you switched to a reduction diet food, as recommended by your vet?
- How much and how often are you feeding your dog? Do you use a measuring cup or just pour food out?
- How many treats do you give your dog every day? What kind?
- Do you give in when your dog begs for table scraps?
- Does more than one person in your household feed your dog?
- Does your dog have access to another pet's food?
- Do you exercise your dog regularly?

The answers may give you some clues as to why and how your dog packed on the pounds. Work with your vet on a diet program for your dog and monitor your dog's weight closely. His life depends on it.

dog weighs the same as he did during his more active years, his muscle-to-fat ratio has changed. Though your dog may have maintained a steady weight of, say, fifty pounds since his young-adult years, the content of those pounds will have changed: the percentage of fat weight increases while the percentage of lean muscle weight decreases.

Your vet may have suggested a feeding protocol, or schedule, along with instructions to include nutraceuticals in your dog's diet. These are fortified food or dietary supplements that provide health benefits in addition to their basic nutritional value. In terms of a feeding schedule or protocol, and based on your dog's individual condition, it might include:

- Reduction in number of calories consumed each day
- A ban on "free feeding," the practice of keeping your dog's bowl or feeder filled at all times so that he can eat whenever he feels like it. Easy for you, but potentially dangerous for him, as this can lead to obesity, especially if your dog is a chowhound.
- More feedings but comprising the same number of calories— two or three smaller meals a day instead of one large one, for example, to increase the energy used to digest those calories
- More or less food per serving, based on number of feedings

In terms of supplements, common dietary additions include glucosamine and chondroitin sulfate to relieve joint, muscle, and bone pain; omega fatty acids for dry skin and skin allergies; vitamin E, as an antioxidant; vitamin C, to boost the immune system; and numerous others. But the same precaution applies here as for prescription medications: never introduce a supplement to your dog's diet without approval from your vet. And be especially careful when you buy dog food, as some of these supplements may already be present in the food. Read the label!

And if your dog's appetite is not what it used to be—common among older dogs—and your vet has confirmed that it is not due to illness or disease or side effects of any medication, he or she may suggest methods to stimulate you dog's flagging interest in food. For example:

- Bring refrigerated food to room temperature before dishing it out (not too long) to let the scent of it emerge and entice your dog.
- Add beef, chicken, or vegetable broth (no sodium, of course) or cooked veggies.
- For serious cases, hand feed your dog.

Everything your vet told you about your dog's nutritional needs will make it much easier to navigate the pet food maze.

Navigating the Food Maze

You know what it's like to stagger down those increasingly long aisles of dog food at the pet superstores, or even your grocery store, wondering how in the world to decide which food to buy your dog. (Commercial pet food is one of the most competitive commodities in the United States.) Perhaps in a moment of weakness you've been swayed by packaging. This is understandable: the $25 billion (worldwide) pet food industry pays its mass-marketers big bucks to learn which colors people prefer, which typefaces and size are easiest and most compelling to read, and which container shapes consumers are drawn to. Because you love your dog and want what's best for him, you want to see past the promotional hoopla and try to interpret what's really in those tempting-sounding packages (can a hard-baked dry pellet *really* taste just like rare roast beef or sirloin steak?). But it's a forest of adjectives out there—"premium," "super-premium," "low-fat," "high-fiber," "senior," "high-protein," "natural," "organic," and on and on—and a lot of pet owners have trouble finding their way through it.

Let's start with some basics.

Pet Food Overview

There are three primary sources of pet food:

- Commercial brands sold in grocery stores
- Commercial pet foods sold in pet stores and pet food supply houses
- Prescription pet foods, available in veterinary offices

Although the commercial selections available in many grocery stores have improved greatly in recent years, most vets agree this source should be your last choice. Understandably, however, many people are tempted to resort to this option for reasons of accessibility and price. Say you've been working late all week, and you're cranky and exhausted and just want to go home and collapse; but you know your cupboards are bare. So, you stop in at a nearby grocery store on your way home; and, while pushing your cart in circles, you realize you're out of dog food, too. And there, oh-so-conveniently located in aisle five, is the store's selection of dog food. And it's so much less expensive than the brands at the pet store. Why not?

The answer, Dr. Richard Goldston says, is in the adage "you get what you pay for." Be particularly wary of generic store brands, as compared with brand names, because the quality of the food's protein can vary greatly even when the ingredients on the label seem to be identical. How is this possible? You have to consider the source. In the higher-quality food, whose protein source is, let's say, chicken or chicken by-products, the meat is likely to be from the breast and legs, whereas in the cheaper food, it may be from the feet, head, and body-cavity contents. Even protein from grain ingredients may be suspect. For example, it may be from "human-quality" cereal grains such as wheat, soybean, or corn, or from moldy, insect-infested grain deemed unfit for human consumption but approved for use in pet foods. Fat content, too, is a cause for concern. You know by now that there are so-called good fats and bad fats. You're

Going Down the Aisle

While the caution against grocery store–brand dog food remains valid generally, it is only fair to note that more "premium" and "stage-of-life" brand dog foods are being sold in grocery stores today. If one that your vet has approved for your dog is available where you shop, by all means, buy it there.

Also note that, according to Dr. Goldston, the higher-quality dog food brands available in grocery stores are always preferable to feeding your dog table foods.

---

also probably all too familiar with the fact that the "bad" fats, the ones to avoid because they're so difficult to digest and high in calories, often are the very ones that make food taste better. The same is true in pet foods. So if you get your dog used to the bad but good-tasting fat in cheaper foods, you're going to have a much more difficult time switching him to a better brand later on when he absolutely must have it to help manage an age-related disease or disorder.

If the older pet is healthy, says Dr. Goldston, as many of them are, many good commercial diets are available for them. "The major pet food companies such as Purina, Iams, Eukanuba, Science, Waltham, and others have a lot of quality products," he says. Here, too, however, you must be careful, as some of these companies also market cheaper foods that may not be adequate for older dogs; but their upper-level diets are very good.

But for older dogs with a specific organ dysfunction such as liver or kidney, or musculoskeletal problems, Dr. Goldston recommends special prescription diets, which he feels are superior to nonprescription choices. These you'll be able to purchase only through your vet. Science Diet has the most types and the longest history of producing very high-quality diets for specific organ dysfunctions, says Dr. Goldston. These include, for example, I/D (intestinal diet), K/D and U/D (kidney failure diets), U/D and S/D (urinary stone diets), R/D and W/D (weight management diets), and L/D (liver failure diet). He adds, however, that Eukanuba, Waltham, Purina, and others also produce very good prescription diets. He cites the Innovative Veterinary Diets (IVD) company as having the best overall selection for treatment of allergies.

Snack Attacks

All this talk about healthy eating may lead you to believe that snacks for your dog are a no-no. Not necessarily. If your dog's snacks are the equivalent of human junk food, get rid of them. But if you feed your dog healthy treats, including fruits and vegetables or vet-approved commercial snacks, you don't have to deprive your dog. One woman who was told to slim down her Labrador retriever after the dog had been diagnosed with arthritis switched from commercial dog treats to carrots and had her dog fit as a fiddle in no time.

The Joy of Cooking for Dogs

A fourth source of dog food is your own kitchen. A growing trend among pet owners is to prepare their dog's food themselves. But before you make this decision, you must consider seriously the investment in time and effort required. First you must learn what makes up a balanced diet for your dog. To be effective, it will have to contain all the right nutrients, in adequate amounts: proteins, fats, grains, vitamins, minerals, and carbohydrates. Meeting this requirement becomes more complicated as he gets older and develops age-related ailments and disorders. And don't forget, you'll have to shop for all these ingredients. Then you must prepare the food; and though you can cook in advance to some degree, this will be an ongoing commitment, 365 days a year. So be honest with yourself or you won't be fair to yourself or your dog. If, for example, you frequently travel on business, is there someone else in your household willing to pick up the spoon and pan in your absence? And if you board your dog at a kennel when you go away, realize that staff there will not be able to offer home-cooked meals in most cases, meaning your dog will be subjected to a sudden change in diet—never a good idea for dogs, especially older ones.

For those willing to make this commitment, however, plenty of help is now available in the form of recipes for dogs. And your vet can give you a jumpstart by detailing the components of a balanced diet for your dog, including supplements.

Some words of caution: Don't, in your enthusiasm, begin by throwing out all the store-bought food you have on the shelf. Again, any diet change must be made gradually. A good plan is to gradually introduce the home-cooked food—two to three times a week, for example. And carefully monitor your dog's appetite and digestion for tolerance: watch for signs of upset, including constipation or diarrhea, gas, belching, vomiting, change in stool, and so on. Bring these changes to the attention of your vet ASAP.

A few books you might want to check out before you make your dog food shopping list include: *Dr. Pitcairn's New Complete Guide to Natural Health for Dogs and Cats* by Richard H. Pitcairn, DVM (Rodale Books, 2005); *The Good Food Cookbook for Dogs: 50 Home-Cooked Recipes for the Health and Happiness of Your Canine Companion* by Donna Twichell Roberts (Quarry Books, 2004); and *Better Food for Dogs: A Complete Cookbook and Nutrition Guide* by David Basin and Jennifer Ashton (Robert Rose, 2002).

In the Raw

A fifth option, feeding your dog raw foods, is somewhat controversial. Proponents contend that cooking and processing destroy important nutrients and that a raw diet most closely resembles how animals eat in the wild. Opponents raise very real safety concerns: uncooked protein may contain deadly microorganisms—for example, chicken and eggs may contain salmonella. And raw foods must be washed thoroughly and stored properly to prevent contamination. This diet also presents the same challenge to the owner as home cooking: you must ensure a proper balance of minerals, protein, vitamins, and so on for your dog to be properly nourished.

Information on this trend is widely available online today. One place to start is the incongruously named BARF, which stands for Biologically Appropriate Raw Food (also, Bones and Raw Food), at www.barfworld.com. There's also the more upbeat-named Bravo, offering "foundation food," at www.bravorawdiet.com. But don't make any decisions about this diet until you talk this over with your vet. Senior dogs' digestive systems tend to be very sensitive, and eating raw just may put them in the rough.

Who's Minding the Store?
Regulating Pet Food

You know if you've ever tried to read a label on a can or bag of dog food that it's not easy to do, even with your reading glasses or one of those handy magnifier strips. Often, there's very little on the list that sounds like, well, real food.

Fortunately, for your dog's health—and your peace of mind—there are some organizations and agencies making an effort to monitor and regulate the content of pet food and, in the case of government agencies, establish standards as to what can and cannot be used in it and what can and cannot be said about it on labels and promotional materials. But you won't be surprised to learn that manufacturers have found ways to get around these standards yet remain within the scope—if not the spirit—of the law.

The details of these efforts are beyond the scope of this book, but the following will give you some background, along with pointers to sources of further information, if you're interested in learning more.

- The U.S. Food and Drug Administration Center for Veterinary Medicine (CVM) regulates the manufacture and distribution of food additives and drugs that will be given to animals. The center is responsible for regulating drugs, devices, and food additives given to, or used on, more than 100 million companion animals (as well as farm animals and other animal species). Go to www.fda.gov/cvm for more on the work of this federal agency.

- The Pet Food Institute (PFI), founded in 1958, calls itself the "voice of U.S. pet food manufacturers," representing the manufacturers of 97 percent of all dog and cat food produced in this country. PFI also serves as the pet food industry's public education and media relations resource, representative before Congress and federal and state agencies, and organizer of seminars and educational programs. Info on the PFI can be found at www.petfoodinstitute.org.

- The Association of American Feed Control Officials (AAFCO) has as its goal to "provide a mechanism for developing and implementing uniform and equitable laws, regulations, standards, and enforcement policies for regulating the manufacture, distribution, and sale of animal feeds." Certainly sounds like a worthwhile undertaking. Unfortunately, its many detractors in the animal welfare world believe its test protocols are weak, hence the AAFCO "guarantee" on pet food labels is unreliable as a guide to pet owners. For more on AAFCO, go to www.aafco.org.

CHECK PLEASE

If you've read this far, it should be clear that there's only one easy answer to which diet you should feed your aging or geriatric dog: the one your vet recommends. Beyond that, a few shopping guidelines may help decide what you ultimately put in your shopping cart, and your dog's bowl:

- The most obvious: check the expiration date.
- Look for the AAFCO guarantee: it may not be perfect, but it's a start.
- Look for "named" meats, such as chicken, lamb, or beef—not the generic "meat." Note the grain content: rice is the most digestible; and be on the lookout for more than one mention of corn.
- Beware the word "meal"—either meat or by-product meal—as the first ingredient listed. These rendered products are the cheapest source of protein, and vary widely in terms of quality and content.
- Ignore such claims as "natural," "light," and "healthy." Neither AAFCO nor the FDA regulates these terms. This is marketing jargon, pure and simple, and it can mean whatever the manufacturer wants it to mean.
- Look for natural preservatives, such as vitamins C and E, and avoid the chemical varieties, which include BHA, BHT, ethoxyquin, and propyl gallate.
- Unless your vet has specifically recommended one, avoid any special or stage-of-life formulas, including "senior" varieties, as they may contain ingredients or supplements not appropriate to your dog's condition.
- Again, avoid the generic store brands, which may be manufacturer rejects in new packaging.

And once you get the food home, here are a few other steps you can take to make sure all's well:

1. When you open the bag, box, or can, sniff it. If it smells rancid, close it back up and return it.
2. To be super safe, transfer dry food to a sealed container; transfer canned food to glass or ceramic containers and refrigerate.

3. To avoid digestion problems, integrate new food in your dog's diet gradually: a ratio of one-third new to two-thirds old is good to start with; increase with a little more new and a little less old food each day.
4. Monitor your dog's acceptance. This includes whether he likes it, how he digests it (watch for gas, belching, or vomiting), and how he eliminates it (check for consistency changes to his stool). Also watch for weight gain or loss and changes to his coat and skin.

One more thing: don't forget the water. Wash out his bowl and put fresh water in it at least once a day, and make sure it's filled at all times.

ON THE EXERCISE TRACK

Exercise is so easy to talk about and so very difficult to actually do. We try every trick in the book to get ourselves going, from paying for membership at a gym to signing up for an exercise class to buying expensive space-hogging equipment for our homes. But too often, the membership goes unused, we skip the class, and the equipment becomes just another place to throw our clothes at the end of the day. We know exercise is vital for maintaining our vigor and controlling our weight, yet our follow-through always seems to fall through. So what can be said here to convince you to exercise your older dog—your sweet, lovable companion of so many years, who has been there for you through thick and thin and never complained, but who needs you now as never before? Will a guilt trip work? It's worth a try.

It is, simply, indisputable that keeping your older dog active both physically and mentally, at whatever level he is capable, for as long as possible, is one of the keys to a long, high-quality life. So if you can't do it for yourself, do it for your dog, and both of you will reap the rewards.

Water Carrier

Don't walk out the door with your dog unless you're packing water and a drinking vessel for him. Pet supply stores now sell handy and compact water bottle/receptacle combinations, making it easy to have water for your dog at all times.

Get the Ball Rolling

Don't even think of starting any exercise program for your older dog before consulting with your vet. This is important if your dog hasn't been doing much lately beyond trundling to his food dish and mustering up just enough energy to welcome you home with a wag when you walk through the door. And it is *imperative* if your dog has mobility problems or has been diagnosed with a disease or dysfunction *of any kind.* As you know for yourself, you can do more harm than good if, in a spurt of enthusiasm and determination, you try to make up for all those nights spent in front of the TV in a single sprint around the park.

Exercise Guidelines

1. *Be sure your dog warms up.* Some dogs make this easy. At the sight of their leash, many dogs begin jumping up and down or going in circles in anticipation of a walk or run. If your dog's mobility is more impaired, however, you'll have to do this for him, by gently bending and stretching his limbs. A stimulating

all-over body rub or massage can do the trick, too. Be gentle with his sore spots and weak areas. Watch him closely: if he winces or yelps, shies away from you, or snaps, it means ease up. When he's ready to go, consider one or more of the following forms of exercise based on your dog's condition and your vet's recommendation:

- *Take a walk: the simplest and still the best exercise for dogs (you, too).* Start slow, especially if your dog hasn't walked farther than the perimeter of his own backyard in a while—five to ten minutes for the first couple of days (or two short walks), then gradually increase, to as much as thirty minutes a day. If possible, stay on grassy surfaces. And be weather conscious: when it's hot or cold, slow the pace and shorten the duration of your walk; in extreme weather, it may be best to exchange the walk for a game of indoor hide-and-seek (see "Play Mind Games," on page 107.

- *Jog, if you and your dog are up to it and your vet gives him the go-ahead.* Again, start slow and, if possible, stay on softer surfaces. And watch your dog carefully: if he starts panting heavily or limping even slightly, stop.

- *Play catch or fetch.* Temper your game to your dog's condition. If your dog has arthritis, for example, pitch the ball low and inside; no high-flies to the outfield. And if your dog has dental problems, his ball-playing days may be over: substitute a softer squeeze toy. Similarly, if your dog used to go by leaps and bounds to retrieve a far-flung Frisbee, bring him down to earth now that he's older.

- *Goof around at home.* When the weather's bad or too hot or cold, get your dog up and at 'em with a gentle wrestling match (roll him over, tussle with him), a game of keepaway (an old sock is good for this), or hide-and-seek with a favorite chew toy.

Old Dogs, Young Kids

Sometimes, there's nothing better for helping an old dog to feel young again than to hang out with a child. But children must be mature enough to follow your guidelines and to understand your dog's limitations. Teach the child to recognize signs from your dog that he's had enough. And keep an eye on them, to ensure they don't go overboard in their enthusiasm.

- *Go for a swim.* This nonimpact exercise is one of the best forms of physical activity for an old dog's limbs and joints. A number of veterinary hospitals now have pools for dogs. Ask your vet if there's one near you. Or, if your dog is small, you may be able to get him in the swim in a bathtub or children's pool. Be aware, though, that older dogs become chilled more quickly, so keep a close eye on him and the water temperature—and never leave him alone in the water.
- *Socialize and exercise at the same time.* If your community has a dog run or park, and your dog is up to the level of interaction, this can be a terrific stimulant, both socially and

physically. You must be cautious and alert at all times, however; so though you may be tempted to bring a newspaper or book to read while your dog frolics, it's best to keep an eye on him. Dogs playing together can become rambunctious, even aggressive.

Tip

Dog parks and dog runs aren't just for city canines anymore; they're everywhere. To find one—or learn how to start one—go to www.dogpark.com, which at the time of this writing was updating its extensive U.S. and Canadian dog park listings.

2. *Don't overdo.* Dogs have the "disease to please," and they'll try to keep up with you even when they shouldn't. If your dog poops out before you do, call it quits. You can finish your own workout later, alone.

3. *Cool down.* If you've been walking or running, slow the pace; then sit in the shade or the sun, depending on the weather, for a few minutes. If your dog has been for a swim, dry him off thoroughly, rubbing gently with a soft, clean towel (don't forget his outer ear canal—more on this in the material on grooming, later in this chapter). If your dog has been cavorting in a dog park or run, sit with him away from the crowd for a few minutes before you leash him and stroll slowly home.

4. *Monitor your dog for signs of stress and exhaustion, weakness, pain, or discomfort.* This is the most important guideline: your dog will tell you when he's had enough—or too much. Pay attention: watch for drooping head and tail; coughing, long-term heavy panting/breathing.

Giving Your Dog a Lift

Even if your dog is more seriously disabled or infirm, he still may be a candidate for modified exercise in the form of *assisted ambulation*, courtesy of a number of inventive devices available on the market. Some offer support for the front legs and chest; others for the hindquarters. If your dog needs a lift, check out these resources:

K-9 Cart Company: Offers custom-made mobility aids for dogs. Veterinary technicians help with type and dimensions. K-9 is the original manufacturer of these devices; the company also offers valuable advice on nursing care for infirm dogs. 800-578-6960 or 866-592-2787; www.k9carts.com

Bottom's Up Leash: Manufactures a rear-end harness that supports your dog's back legs and hindquarters, while it transfers the weight to you, as you hold the leash. (Read "Watson's Story" below to learn how this leash came to be.) 800-805-2001; www.bottomsupleash.com

Dewey's Wheelchairs for Dogs: Provides custom-made wheelchairs for dogs that have lost the use of their hind legs. Dewey's also makes wheelchairs for quadriplegic dogs. 877-312-2122; www.wheelchairsfordogs.com

Eddie's Wheels: Offers another source for wheelchairs, but this company also makes available refurbished chairs, when money *is* an object. 888-211-2700; www.eddieswheels.com

Drs. Foster & Smith: Offers a complete range of products for senior pets, including mobility and access devices. This is also a good source for lower-priced, vet-approved pharmaceuticals. 800-381-7179; www.drsfostersmith.com

This is just a get-you-started list of sources for canine mobility aids. You will find many more online by typing search terms such as: "handicapped dogs," "dog wheelchairs," "senior dog products," or "dogs with disabilities." Definitely do some comparison shopping, as many of these devices do not come cheap. Wheelchairs, in particular, can run in the hundreds of dollars, as they must be custom-made.

WATSON'S STORY: BOTTOM'S UP

Watson came to live with me when he was just about eight weeks old; he was the runt of the litter. He was part sheepdog and part Lab, and I always joked that he liked to be known as a sheepador. Runt or not, he knew he was adorable, and together we played on that.

Watson and I went everywhere together: to my ballgames, to the beach, to the park. I treasured all those moments that I spent with him. Routinely every morning I would get up and fix Watson his breakfast first. I loved to sing to him—anything from made-up songs to songs using his name in appropriate spots. Watson would sit there, looking up at me, happy with any interaction. It was exciting just to come home and see him. I could not wait to take him down to the beach or to the schoolyard and run him in his younger days. He was such a wiseguy. Our walks were always something special. When a person walks his dog, a complete bonding takes place. It is not just for the animal to relieve himself or to get a little bit of exercise. It is so much more than that: it is spiritual.

When the wildfires ravaged southern California in 1993, I was away from my home when my area started to burn. I remember so clearly making a deal with "the man upstairs," promising him that if he gave me Watson, he could burn the house straight to the ground and I would

Watson and Arnie: a dynamic duo

consider it even. That is exactly what happened. It is still one of the best deals that I have ever made.

I remember, too, the day I began to notice that Watson had started to slow down. It was the first sad sign I had that he was getting older. Then he had the first of his seizures—how frightened both of us were. I tried to block out the obvious and make myself believe it was a onetime occurrence. But it didn't work, and I started to worry about him all the time; no matter where I was, if he was not with me, I feared something might happen to him. I child-proofed the house, blocking off all of the stairs so that he could not go up them and possibly fall down.

When Watson was fifteen years old he became afflicted with arthritis and hip dysplasia. He had a great deal of difficulty getting up and walking, so I would carry him. People would come up to me and tell me what a great owner I was. My reply was, "No, not really, I just have a phenomenal dog."

I tried everything to help Watson—acupuncture, medications. But nothing was really working, and I knew that I would have to find a way to continue walking Watson, whether it meant carrying him around or finding some other way.

Then one night, watching a show on rock climbing, I focused on those harnesses they use to haul themselves up, and I got the idea that I might be able to make a sling for Watson's rear end. I went to a pet store, bought five leashes, cut them up, and sewed them so that I was able to slip the contraption over his tush and support his rear end. It must have looked quite funny to other people, but both Watson and I enjoyed the attention. More than the attention, though, I started getting inquiries from people asking where they could purchase what eventually became known as the Bottom's Up Leash. For Watson's part, he seemed to know that this invention was his, that it carried his stamp of approval.

When I realized that the end was near, I would look up toward the heavens and plead, "Please do not make me do your job." But in the end I had to. He was seventeen when he died, but he was my baby to the end. Every day I think of him. His pictures adorn my whole house and my office. I loved all my dogs, but Watson was that special one.

The legacy of Watson is the creation of the Bottom's Up Leash. He lives on through so many animals that have been helped by "his" invention. I have been told that he winks every time I sell a leash. As for me, I am very fortunate that now I get to talk about Watson every single day, because he is involved in my business. In essence, it is his business. My partner believes we should give away the Bottom's Up Leash for free and just charge for the Watson stories. I have a million of them. We all have a million stories that we can tell about the precious creatures that come into our lives and touch us so.

—*Arnie Costell, Santa Monica, California*

Go into Training

It may seem an unlikely recommendation, but obedience training or behavior counseling is a viable form of exercise for senior dogs. And, yes, you can teach an old dog new tricks; in fact, many old dogs make better students than the puppy crowd. This is also a good way to address any bad behavior your old boy has been exhibiting as a result of not feeling well. In particular, if your dog has become snappish lately, and you have young children, a qualified trainer may just be able to offer the solution.

Take care, though, to seek out a certified trainer or counselor working in a gentle, stress-free environment—ideally, someone who understands the special needs of older dogs. Now is not the time for intensive boot camp. Ask for a personal referral from your vet or a fellow dog lover, then see if you can audit a class or counseling session before you sign up your dog.

Play Mind Games

As important as it is to exercise your dog's body, it's just as vital to keep him mentally stimulated. Says Dr. Goldston, "Mental stimulation greatly improves both the longevity and quality of life of all senior dogs." Failure to do so, he adds, leads to a great increase in obsessive compulsive disorder (OCD). The most common form of canine OCD is called *lick granuloma*, where the dog begins to obsessively lick a certain area on his front or back legs. The more he licks, the more it itches, the more he licks . . . The result is a thick sore that can become infected, further aggravating the licking behavior.

Get Some Therapy

Modern veterinary care now includes physical therapy, or rehabilitation, for dogs recovering from surgery or other major treatment protocols, to improve mobility, strength, and stamina. Hydrotherapy is especially popular, and a number of facilities are now open nationwide. These are also excellent exercise options for dogs that need more careful monitoring and very gentle handling. Go to www.handicappedpets.com, to find rehabilitation facilities listed by state.

Mental exercise may also help slow the progression of Cognitive Dysfunction Syndrome (CDS) in dogs showing early signs of that mentally debilitating disease.

How do you mentally stimulate a dog? If your dog has enough mobility, the best way is to use some form of controlled exercise for which they have to use their senses of sight, smell, and hearing. (And, note, though many aging dogs lose their sight or hearing, it's less likely for them to lose their sense of smell.) Hide-and-seek is a good option, with either a person or a favorite toy, as is a game of fetch. Be lavish with the praise, or provide a healthy treat when your dog succeeds, to reinforce the activity.

Dr. Goldston is a strong proponent of introducing a puppy or young dog to households with an older dog. He says, "I universally advise clients that have dogs entering their senior years to get a new puppy. By far the best activity for mentally stimulating senior and geriatric dogs is the near-constant harassment from a young puppy." It has the added benefit, he says, of helping to ease the owner's pain of loss when the older pet dies.

Young children can be just as effective in keeping an old dog on his toes, but as mentioned on page 101, in "Old Dogs, Young Kids," they must be given a clear list of do's and don'ts and told how to recognize signs of weariness or discomfort in the dog.

Oh, yes, did we mention love? Serve it up, and plenty of it. Dr. Goldston says that probably the most effective mental stimulation for less mobile pets is when owners take time each day to pet, scratch, rub, talk—just interact with their dog.

ATTENDING TO THE OUTER DOG

With your dog properly fed and exercised, you can't really expect him to walk around in that scruffy old coat now, can you? Jokes aside, you must not. For senior dogs, grooming is not optional. Older dogs that are not groomed regularly are at greater risk for succumbing to parasite-borne diseases, ear and eye infections, skin and other cancers, and tooth and gum disease (the latter of which can turn much more serious, even deadly). Grooming your dog is one of *the* best ways to catch signs of problems before they turn serious. Your hands-on attention will lead you to discover early: lumps, tumors, or other skin formations; sores and cuts; skin parasites; hair loss; tender body parts; tooth decay and gum discoloration; and dry, cracked footpads or nails. Grooming is also the ideal way to show your dog love and affection—vital ingredients to his sense of well-being.

Senior dogs typically need grooming more often than younger ones; in most cases, they should receive daily attention. A groomer may be in order for major cleanings and clippings, especially if yours is a long-haired breed or a very large dog difficult for you to handle alone; but you need to stay involved. It doesn't take long to "run a comb through his hair"; and in the long run, doing so will save you money in between checkup trips to the vet and professional grooming sessions.

To help you commit to this aspect of your dog's health care regime, you might consider preassembling a grooming kit and assigning a time each day for the task (for example, when you sit down to listen to the news).

GROOMING KIT COMPONENTS

- Brush and comb appropriate for your dog's hair type and length and skin condition. Your vet or a professional groomer can give you guidance, then spend some time reading labels on the grooming shelves of your favorite pet supply store.
- Shampoo specially formulated for your senior dog's sensitive skin (no human products, please!); and, perhaps, dry shampoo for cold-weather days or when your dog is feeling poorly
- Lots of large, soft towels

- Handheld shower attachment
- Portable basin and washcloths, if a full bath is not an option
- Nail clippers
- Scissors, to cut away matted hair or trapped debris from outdoors
- No-slip bathmat or washable rug
- Cotton balls, to put in his ears and to wipe away tear deposits
- Dog-formulated toothbrush and toothpaste (the human variety causes stomach upset)

Brushing and Bathing

There's no one right way to bathe a dog. So many factors are involved: the dog's size and weight, hair length and type; his state of health; his attitude toward bath time (those runaway, sopping-wet dog stories are not just the stuff of fiction). And what about you? How well can you manage your dog? Is your dog a giant and you a petite? How's your back? Can you get a squirming, soaking-wet, sensitive senior in and out of a tub without damage to either

---

One Bath to Go, Please

Not everyone can do the "heavy lifting" required to thoroughly bathe a senior dog, especially one that needs special handling. If you and your dog have grown old together, for example, and you have your own health and mobility issues to consider, help may be just around the corner. Many communities across the country today, especially those with large retirement populations, offer mobile grooming services for pets. Some will pick up, groom, and return your dog to you smelling like a rose (well, not exactly); others will groom your dog in your home. Your vet may know of such a service; and, often, these groomers-on-the-go advertise their services in neighborhood newspapers and pet supply stores.

Body Check

When your dog's hair is still wet or damp, it is the best time to check his skin for any growths, sores, or cuts. Don't rely on just a visual: run your hands up and down, over and under. If you see or feel something of concern, make a mental or written note of where exactly it is, because it's often much more difficult to relocate when your dog is dry.

one of you? The point is, you'll have to find a way that works for both of you. It's a good idea to consult with your vet about this, too. You may find that sponge baths are the most effective. They work in hospitals for human patients, why not dogs, patient or otherwise? Dry shampooing is also an option.

Your dog's bathing needs will also be dictated in part by his type of coat and undercoat (whether short or long, oily or dry, thin or dense) and whether he is out and about in the great outdoors on a regular basis.

It's a good idea to brush or comb your dog before you get him wet. You'll get rid of a lot of dry debris, comb out tangles and mats that would only get worse when wet, and relax your dog (unless he's one of those who balks under the brush).

Whether your dog will get all-over wet in a tub or in patches from a sponge bath, use comfortably warm, not hot, water. Likewise the room temperature. Soap him up gently and thoroughly (don't forget his feet), and rinse well. Don't get so caught up in the washing process that you forget to be mindful of your dog's body temperature. If he starts shivering, get him out and dry immediately.

Wrap a towel around him to absorb as much water as possible before he manages to free himself to do the "shimmy-shake." Finish the job when he settles down. If your dog has long, and especially fine, hair, blot—don't rub—or you'll cause tangles. If you do rub, be gentle.

Brushing your dog daily is one of the best things you can do for him, and it can extend the time between baths. You stimulate oil production to the skin, remove dead skin and loose hair, and keep dander under control. Brush down to the roots, taking care not to be too rough. If your dog has short or thin hair, you won't need to apply as much force as for dogs with thick, long, or curly hair. And if your dog has any harmless growths (which you know because your vet told you), such as common fatty tumors called lipomas, or warts, be very careful not to aggravate them with the brush, as they can bleed and become infected.

Teeth and Gums

As you learned in Chapter 3, brushing your dog's teeth and gums is one of the most important steps you can take to ensure your dog's long life and good health. Periodontal disease, left untreated, can

lead to tooth loss and, in the worst case, infection of major organs including the lungs, kidneys, and liver—even the nervous system—and, eventually, to death (more on this in Chapter 6). Sadly, too few pet owners include brushing their dog's teeth and gums as part of their grooming process, making periodontal disease the most common clinical condition in companion animals, according to the American Veterinary Dental College (AVDC).

It's unclear why so many pet owners neglect this aspect of their dog's care; perhaps it seems too unwieldy or uncomfortable a task. But it's very important to learn, especially for older dogs. The less often your dog has to be anesthetized for full cleanings or other dental work, the better. Your vet or veterinary technician can show you the proper way, and can give you the proper tools. You'll need a pet-formula toothpaste (made to be swallowed, because dogs can't spit) and toothbrush. You might need someone to help control your dog at first, if you've never done this before. Here are three simple getting-started guidelines for those who have never gone hand-to-mouth with their pooch before:

1. Don't use the toothbrush at first: instead, use your index finger, to rub your dog's gums, front to back. To make this more palatable to him, literally, wrap your finger in gauze, then dip it in some broth before you start.
2. Now try it with the toothbrush, inserting it gently under his cheek. Talk quietly to your dog as you go, to calm him. Don't force it, or he'll never become accustomed to the procedure.
3. For the first few attempts, keep the sessions short.
4. If at first you don't succeed, try, try again.

Your vet may recommend you begin feeding your dog a plaque-and-tartar-control food, and add an oral hygiene chew to your dog's diet. You might also investigate some of the newer plaque prevention products on the market, which are designed to help slow plaque buildup, which is the beginning of dental disease.

National Pet Dental Health Month

Funded by an educational grant from Hill's Pet Nutrition, Inc., the American Veterinary Medical Association (AVMA) and the American Veterinary Dental Society (AVDS) team up each February to launch a consumer awareness campaign, designed to stress the importance of regular dental care for pets.

Ears

The moist inner areas of your dog's ears are prime real estate for mites, bacteria, even yeast infections. To prevent them from moving into the neighborhood, include ear cleaning as part of your grooming procedure. You'll need cotton balls and/or swabs and some ear cleanser from your vet. This is a fairly simple procedure: you squeeze a little cleanser into his ear (not too much or when he shakes his head, as he inevitably will, most of it will end up on you), fold the earflap down, and hold it for a minute or so, then clean up the excess from the backside of the ear and around the perimeter of the outer canal. (Do not go too deep into the canal; you risk doing damage by putting bacteria on the express train to the inner ear.) Those of you with floppy-eared breeds will need to be more conscientious about ear care.

Nails

Overnight: that's how fast an old dog's nails seem to grow. And they're more brittle than they used to be. You'll have to be attentive to stay on top of your dog's nail care, but fortunately, you'll get clear clues when he's due for a pedicure. Two common signs are the tell-tale clicking sound across a bare floor and snagging in carpeted areas (your dog may stop dead in his tracks when one of his claws gets hooked in a carpet loop). Allowed to grow too long, a dog's claws may curl around themselves and can puncture his footpads, causing infection. The rule of thumb is to keep nails short enough so that when your dog is standing still they do not touch the ground.

Nail clipping can be fast and painless—for both of you—if this has been a regular part of your grooming regime over the years and you're comfortable using either the standard nail clippers or a tool commonly called a "grinder." But for a lot of people, this is something best left to the pros, either because their dogs are too big for them to manage easily or because their dogs have very tough, thick nails. It doesn't cost a lot, and takes just seconds, to bring your dog to one of the pet superstores with on-site grooming facilities, and have his nails clipped there. Your vet can do it, too, during a check-up; and, certainly, all groomers offer this service.

And while you're "playing footsie" with your dog, take out the pair of small scissors from your grooming kit and trim the hair between his nails. This little extra tidying up will go a long way to preventing foot injuries caused when thorns, debris, even glass, get trapped in the hair down there.

SUMMARY

There is no way to measure the value of the bond you have with your dog. Most people would say they have no words to describe it. As your dog ages, and your involvement in his care becomes more intense, that bond deepens further still. By providing your dog with proper nutrition, appropriate exercise, and regular grooming, you will be solidifying that bond at the same time you are ensuring a high quality of life for him.

KEY PET POINTS

- With guidance from your vet, shop carefully for your dog's food. Do not be penny wise and pound foolish: cheaper food is almost always of poorer quality, and you'll pay for it in the long run when you have to address diet-related health problems in your dog.

- Keeping your dog active, both physically and mentally, is essential for his well-being over the long term. There are exercise options and aids available today even for dogs that are seriously disabled or infirm.

- Proper grooming (including brushing his teeth) not only makes your dog feel good and look good, it's one of the best ways to keep him in good health. It also helps you to stay on top of any changes to his body, so that they can be addressed early, when treatment options are most effective.

- Always follow your vet's recommendations for feeding, exercising, and grooming your dog. Too much is at stake to do otherwise.

CHAPTER 6

When Your Dog Gets Sick: Understanding Common Age-Related Ailments and Their Treatments

Dogs and humans share a remarkable emotional bond that every dog lover knows and cherishes. We also have a lot in common when it comes to how our bodies work—and, ultimately, falter. "I believe," says Dr. Richard Goldston, "there is a much greater difference between a dog and a cat than there is between a dog and a human as far as physiology and pharmacology are concerned." Recently, for example, close parallels have been identified between the cognitive changes in an aging dog's brain and those of the human brain. Research in cognitive dysfunction syndrome in dogs may help scientists better understand Alzheimer's disease in humans.

It is not surprising, then, that many of the diseases and ailments common to the aging dog also occur in their human companions. In this chapter, you will get a brief overview of a number of the ailments prevalent among the senior and geriatric dog population, and you may recognize a number of them as commonplace among humans as well. Some of the diagnostic tools and treatment protocols may also sound familiar. But as closely linked to humans as dogs are, there are differences—in how they respond to certain treatments and drugs, for example, and how they experience pain. Therefore, tempting as it may be—because we feel so close to our dogs and know them so well—it is unwise to *anthropomorphize*—to assign human feelings to our dogs when they are sick. Rely on your vet to give you the details you need to understand how your dog may be experiencing her illness or treatment.

Another word of caution: reading through a list of disease descriptions is unsettling, to say the least. Therefore, a good idea is to just skim through these sections, taking special note of the symptoms given in the "At a Glance" boxes. If something raises a red flag, read more closely; if you're still concerned, call your vet. Don't jump to conclusions. The key here is to inform, not scare, yourself.

As you read about what can go wrong, keep in mind that advances in veterinary medicine can, in many cases, help things go right again—no, not forever, but for longer than previously possible. Today's veterinarians and veterinary specialists can routinely offer treatments that, not too long ago, were reserved for the human animal—including pacemakers, kidney transplants, joint replacements, radiation and chemotherapy, sophisticated testing protocols, and much, much more. (Of course, these high-level treatments come at a price, a health care issue we'll address in the next chapter.)

CHOOSING TREATMENT PROTOCOLS

In reading about these age-related diseases and conditions, you'll note in many cases that more than one type of treatment may be appropriate. It will be up to you, the pet owner, in close consult with your vet, to decide how you want to proceed. A number of factors will go into your decision-making process, some of which may include:

- Your dog's specific diagnosis
- Her prognosis (her prospect of recovery) and her quality of life as a sick dog
- Your health care preferences (Do you tend to have the most faith in the latest drug treatments, for example, or do you always prefer to take an alternative approach, such as acupuncture, if one's available and appropriate?)
- The cost of the recommended treatment and your budget (Can you afford it?)

- The amount and type of care your dog requires (Do you have the time? Are you prepared to give shots, clean wounds, deal with drug side effects, and so on—perhaps for an extended period of time?)

There may be many other factors, based on your individual lifestyle and circumstances. In its "Senior Care Guidelines for Dogs and Cats," the American Animal Hospital Association (AAHA) recommends that its member veterinarians always tell their clients *all* the best options, even those the vet believes the client will decline. "The veterinarian," the guidelines state, "has a responsibility to *recommend* what is best for the pet, but the *chosen* treatment must be what is best for both the patient and the client." To that end, your vet should:

1. Explain all the consequences of each available choice, including your responsibilities and all related costs in time and money.
2. Design a treatment protocol that best enables you to comply with it. Will you be able to administer twice daily shots to your diabetic dog, for example, or give daily subcutaneous injections to your dog in renal failure? If not, alternative approaches should be discussed.
3. Detail all side effects and quality-of-life issues associated with the treatment of choice.
4. Back up verbal instructions with clear written documentation. Offer training, if necessary, in treatment delivery.
5. Explain how to monitor your dog's response to the chosen treatment. Typically you will be asked to log any side effects or complications you notice, including behavioral changes. This will be especially important if your dog is taking more than one medication, when drug interactions must be closely tracked. Doing so will help your vet adjust dosages or switch or discontinue drugs.

It is when your dog is sick that your partnership with your vet becomes most meaningful. To give your dog the best care available, your vet will be counting on you to supply the information necessary. This is one reason it is a good idea to have established a rapport with your vet earlier on, during wellness checkups. Looking for the right vet when your dog is ill will only add stress.

Types of Treatment: Definition of Terms

In the next section, which describes a number of conditions common to aging dogs, you'll see in many cases more than one type of treatment listed. Some are considered traditional, others are alternative. It's important to understand what those terms mean in a medical context.

"Traditional" is the word used by both health care practitioners and consumers to mean the established or customary way of treating illness and disease, as taught in most medical school curricula in this country. Traditional medicine includes various testing and exploratory procedures for diagnosis purposes, surgeries, therapeutic drug treatments, and so on. In addition to traditional approaches, a number of alternative treatment choices are available to pet owners and veterinary practitioners. Most of these are options also available in human health care.

Tip: Keep a Treatment Log

A small notebook is good for this. A memo calendar is even better, where you can keep track of the dates of treatments, along with your dog's reactions and responses. It's a good idea to keep the calendar in the same place you keep your dog's medication or other treatment instructions, to remind you to update it. And when you check in with your vet, by phone or in person, have the calendar in hand.

In the context of medical care, "alternative" just means "another," "unconventional," or "nonstandard" treatment. It does not mean not as good; it just means different. Whether an alternative choice for medical treatment is better or worse than a traditional approach depends on a number of factors: the medical condition being treated; the professional delivering the treatment; whether other treatments are being given; at what stage during the disease or illness treatment began; and many others. The same potential for success exists whether you choose a traditional or alternative treatment method for your dog.

Give Me an Alternative

If you are interested in learning more about alternative approaches to traditional veterinary practice or want to find a vet specializing in alternative and holistic treatments, go to the Web site www.alternativesforanimals.com.

A hydrotherapy session at the Center for Specialized Veterinary Care, Westbury, New York, home to the Compassionate Care Center, the first animal hospital in the world where pet owners can spend the night with their sick pets. Seven rooms, complete with sleeping accommodations for both pets and people, Internet access, and televisions, Dr. Diane Levitan developed the center to "increase awareness of the pet as part of the family."

Call for Regulation

Though Dr. Goldston believes there is a place for holistic medicine in animal care, he sees a major problem. Currently, unlike for traditional medications, there are no regulations to ensure the purity and volume of active ingredients in holistic medicines. Alternative medicines are considered dietary supplements or nutrients, not pharmaceuticals, thus there are no federal or state regulatory bodies such as the Federal Drug Administration (FDA) or the United States Department of Agriculture (USDA) to monitor content claims.

The term "alternative medicine" came into use around 1977, to describe various systems of healing or treating disease. It is usually thought to include acupuncture, traditional Chinese medicine (TCM), chiropractic, homeopathy, herbal treatments, even faith healing, and others. Typically, these are not included in the traditional medical curricula taught in the United States—though this has been changing slowly in recent years. Interestingly, some alternative treatments, such as acupuncture, have been in use for thousands of years longer than traditional medicine.

Finally, there's "integrative medicine," a newer term in the medical lexicon. It simply means to coordinate, incorporate, or blend two or more treatment options into a protocol as appropriate for a given condition and a given patient. Many veterinary practitioners today favor this approach. Dr. Goldston says, "The ideal situation to me is definitely an integrative approach. The only definite wrong to me is to only rely on conventional veterinary medicine *or* alternative veterinary medicine 100 percent of the time." As you'll read in the conclusion to "Gus's Story" here, an integrated approach to animal care can be very successful.

THE CONCLUSION OF GUS'S STORY:
ON PINS AND NEEDLES

A few weeks after Gus had been diagnosed with inter-vertebral disk disease (IVDD) and had begun taking prednisone, my sister called to ask how he was feeling. "Not very well," was my response. She asked if I had ever considered taking an alternative avenue of treatment, such as acupuncture. She had heard it was particularly effective in treating back injuries. Since Gus had not been respond-

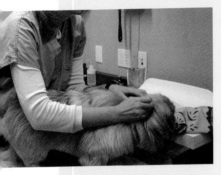

ing well to traditional medicine, I decided to follow up on her suggestion. I am so glad I did.

I contacted both my regular veterinarian and my dog groomer. Each provided me with several names. Based on interviews I conducted over the phone, I chose the San Francisco Veterinary Specialists, even though it meant an almost two-hour round-trip drive from where we live, south of the city. On that first visit, after the vets there concurred with the original diagnosis, Gus was given his first acupuncture treatment. Needles were placed in his neck, his spinal area, his hindquarters, and his feet. He was a real trooper and fussed minimally, dislodging only one

Acupuncture put Gus back on his feet again.

needle from his right front paw. The vet also prescribed two herbs, AC-Q Tabs (for joint and muscle pain, accompanied by weakness of the legs, hips, and back) and Resinall-E Tabs (for swelling and pain due to traumatic injuries). In addition, we were encouraged to decrease the prednisone to 2.5mg once daily, with the goal of completely eliminating the prednisone from his system, as he wasn't tolerating the steroid well at all.

As amazed as I was that he had accepted the needles so willingly, more astonishing to me was that after only one treatment he was able to stand on all fours again! He still couldn't walk well, but—and this is a big but—he was upright on his own.

We made another acupuncture appointment for the following week, and the week after that, and the week after that . . . The vet-acupuncturist calculated two months of weekly treatments, with the eventual goal of once a month. Though finding space in a very tight budget for another $400 a month took some creative accounting, watching Gus continually improve was more than worth the monetary sacrifice.

The first thing we noticed was how bright and shiny his eyes were getting. They looked like puppy eyes. Next we saw improvement in his ability to stand on the slippery kitchen floor, and finally even to dig in our backyard. I was so happy to see him having fun in the dirt, I didn't even scold him for his excavations. It was like watching my dog return from the land of the zombies. The more acupuncture he received, the less prednisone he took, and the stronger he became.

Gus is now having acupuncture treatments once a month. He no longer takes prednisone but is still on the herbal formula AC-Q. Rarely, we use a support sling harness with a handle to assist him on his daily jaunts around the neighborhood, but it is still necessary to carry him up and down the stairs to avoid reinjury.

In spite of all his progress, however, for a while I still found myself worrying, especially when I stayed out late: Would he try to climb the stairs and get stuck, unable to go either up or down? Would I arrive home to find him in pain because I wasn't available when he needed me? I was becoming neurotic with what-ifs. More recently I've come to accept that no matter how conscientious I am at attempting to shield my "Funny Face" from pain, there is only a limited amount of time he will be with us. I can either choose to enjoy and revel in our shared life with him or constantly fear the worst. So I'm learning to celebrate the time we have together.

When the moment comes to release Gus, we plan to have him euthanized, at home, and bury him close to his sister, Cider, who passed away several years ago.

Until that time, I'm trying to keep my promise to him and find something every day that I can celebrate. It's working. I feel more at peace within myself, more balanced and ready to both face the challenges and accept the opportunities that present themselves. After all, as Gus has taught me, all I have to do is concentrate and put one foot in front of the other.

Contact Point

For more information on animal acupuncture, and to find a specialist in your area, go to the American Holistic Veterinary Medical Association (AHVMA) Web site: www.ahvma.org.

You as a pet owner have access to all these forms of treatment for your dog. Which you choose will depend on your understanding of which approach has the best chance of success, your preferences for or against traditional versus alternative treatments, cost, and so on.

By the Letter

For convenience, the diseases and conditions listed in this section are given in alphabetical order.

DISEASES AND CONDITIONS COMMON AMONG AGING DOGS

The list of diseases and conditions given here is far from comprehensive; it is intended only to introduce you to a number of the health issues your dog may face as she ages. This material is supplied only for informational purposes: only a certified veterinarian, performing the requisite exams and tests, can properly diagnose and treat a sick animal. If your dog is displaying symptoms of illness of any kind, make an appointment with your vet as soon as possible.

Arthritis

More properly called osteoarthritis, this degenerative joint and cartilage disease is very common in aging dogs but is more widely seen in large and giant breeds. It is frequently accompanied by hip dysplasia (see below). Together these two ailments can seriously impair your dog's mobility—and her quality of life. Caused in most cases by simple wear to bones and joints over time, arthritis often occurs at points of previous injury or when there's a history of infection such as Lyme disease.

Keeping your dog in shape through regular exercise and proper nutrition are your best lines of defense against this painful disease, as well as your best approach after your dog has been diagnosed (see Chapter 5). When it comes to treatment, many pet owners and vets take a truly integrative approach, combining prescription medications such as nonsteroidal anti-inflammatory drugs (NSAIDs) with supplements and alternative treatments such as acupuncture. Or they may switch between them, as the effectiveness of one treatment begins to wear off.

AT A GLANCE: ARTHRITIS

Symptoms	Diagnosis	Treatment(s)
Stiffness; difficulty getting up and down; limping or favoring one leg; whimpering or yelping on sudden movement; licking sore limb/joint	Physical exam of affected limb(s); possibly X-rays	Nonsteroidal anti-inflammatory drugs (NSAIDs); neutraceuticals such as glucosamine and chondroitin sulfate; acupuncture, hydrotherapy, massage; dietary adjustments, especially to reduce weight and pressure on affected limbs/joints; surgery

Cancer

It's the dreaded "C" word, the one every pet owner hopes they never will hear. But, today, cancer does not automatically mean a death sentence. As with the human disease, some canine cancers can be cured, others managed to extend life and offer quality of life. Though all cancers have in common abnormal, uncontrollable cell growth that destroys normal, healthy tissue, cancer is not a single disease; it takes many forms, some more dangerous than others.

AT A GLANCE: CANCER, GENERALLY

Symptoms	Diagnosis	Treatment(s)
Abnormal swellings/ growths; sores that don't heal; weakness or shortness of breath; difficulty eating or swallowing, loss of appetite and weight loss; bleeding or discharge from any body openings; problems urinating/ defecating	Depending on the symptoms: aspiration and/or biopsy, for external growths; imaging tools such as X-rays, ultrasound, and magnetic resonance imaging (MRI); exploratory surgery for internal tumors; consultation with veterinary oncologist (cancer specialist)	Depending on the diagnosis: surgery, chemotherapy, radiation; nutritional and holistic therapies

Some of the cancers prevalent among aging and geriatric dogs include the following:

- *Lymphoma*: Lymphoma is a rapidly growing malignancy of the body's lymph system, which includes virtually every organ in the body. The first sign is one or more suspicious lumps, with no accompanying symptoms of illness. Diagnosis involves, typically, a physical exam of the lump(s), blood tests and a urinalysis, and biopsy or aspiration of one or more lymph nodes. Lymphoma is a "staged" disease, meaning it is classified in stages of severity, in this case, I through V, with Stage I being the least severe. Early-stage lymphoma can be managed for months or longer with chemotherapy.

- *Osteosarcoma*: This is bone cancer, usually striking the limbs of larger breeds. It is a fast-spreading tumor, which by the time it has been found in the limb is considered to have already spread. Eventually, it metastasizes (spreads) to the lungs. Primary signs are lameness and tenderness of the affected area, which become progressively worse as the disease develops, causing severe pain. X-rays are used for diagnosis, or a tiny section of bone can be removed for laboratory analysis. Recommended treatment is amputation of the affected bone, followed by chemotherapy or radiation to limit the spread of any cancer cells.

- *Hemangiosarcoma.* This is a malignant tumor of blood vessel cells, striking three areas in particular: the skin, spleen, and heart. Only the skin form can be cured, by surgery, if caught early. As in people, the skin form of this cancer is associated with sun exposure. At highest risk are thin-haired or light-colored dogs, such as Dalmatians. Otherwise, hemangiosarcoma is almost always terminal, as it is associated with serious internal bleeding and rapid internal spread. Treatment can offer only temporary respite. Depending on the type of hemangiosarcoma, diagnosis is through biopsy, chest X-rays, ultrasound of the belly and spleen, and ultrasound of the heart.

- *Mammary (breast) cancer.* As frightening as the statistics for this disease are in women (one in seven or eight), they're even more alarming in female dogs: one in four unspayed female dogs is affected. The key word here is "unspayed." And the more heat cycles she has before you get your dog spayed, the greater the risk she will develop breast cancer. The primary sign to watch for are lumps in the mammary glands that are firm to the touch, especially in the area of the back legs. Many of these tumors will be found to be benign—but they all must be tested. Testing may be done preliminarily through needle aspiration, used to withdraw some cells from the growth for lab evaluation, and ultimately via a biopsy to confirm diagnosis.

Spay to Prevent Cancer

Even if your older dog is already in a high-risk group for breast cancer (e.g., she's older, unspayed, and has had puppies), it doesn't mean you shouldn't have her spayed now. Spaying at any age can help prevent tumor formation.

Anesthetizing the Older Dog

I n the past, many vets simply refused to anesthetize old, and especially sick, dogs. Thanks to new types of anesthesia and procedures, it is safer today. But it is still a risky business and must be approached with caution. Your vet will perform a thorough workup to determine whether your dog is strong enough to be anesthetized.

Before agreeing to any procedure that will require your dog to be anesthetized, make sure your vet explains in detail all the risks involved, as well as the benefits. As for human patients, veterinarians will ask you to sign "informed consent" forms for all procedures.

CANCER TREATMENTS

The most widely used cancer treatments are surgery, chemotherapy, radiation, and, in a supporting role, nutrition.

- *Surgery*: Sometimes invasive treatments are performed to remove a cancerous tumor or other malignant growth, partially or entirely, depending on the location of the growth. Surgery is often supplemented with chemotherapy or radiation, for insurance or to attack cancer cells that could not be removed surgically.

- *Chemotherapy*: This is simply drug therapy, as opposed to surgery or radiation. Powerful drugs are administered in a series of injections to kill cancer cells or slow their growth. It's important to note that animals typically do not suffer the serious side effects that humans do while undergoing chemotherapy: Few suffer hair loss (though some lose their whiskers) and few develop infection or experience nausea. Rarely do they have to be hospitalized due to side effects of the medications. Older dogs, however, generally have lower tolerance to these powerful drugs.

- *Radiation:* The objective of radiation is to aim powerful X-rays at the cancerous growth or area, ideally sparing healthy tissue around it. It is typically used for cases of inoperable cancers or to supplement surgery. Dogs receiving radiation may develop soreness in their mouths, making it difficult for them to eat, just when they need nutrition most (in which case, special feeding regimens may be required).

- *Nutritional therapy:* Loss of appetite is common among canine cancer patients, and weight loss and corresponding weakness can seriously affect how well they respond to their primary cancer treatment. It is important, therefore, to talk to your vet about special diets, supplements, and ways to tempt your dog to eat while she's undergoing treatment for cancer.

Cancer Information and Support

Sadly, cancer is one of the most commonly diagnosed diseases in senior dogs, especially those over ten years of age. As a positive consequence of that sad statistic, there's an abundance of information and support available. In addition to consultations with your vet and, if called for, a veterinary oncologist, you may want to do further research on your own, or connect with other pet owners whose dogs have cancer. Three good places to start are:

- Canine Cancer Awareness: www.caninecancerawareness.org
- Veterinary Cancer Society: www.vetcancersociety.org
- Perseus Foundation: www.perseusfoundation.org

Cognitive Dysfunction Syndrome (CDS)

Cognitive dysfunction syndrome (also called canine cognitive dysfunction), the canine version of Alzheimer's disease, has been mentioned several times throughout this book. As with

Alzheimer's, CDS is very disturbing to witness: suddenly your dog doesn't seem like your dog anymore—especially if she seems to no longer recognize you or the members of your family.

Her behavior may also change dramatically—a sweet-natured dog may become uncharacteristically aggressive or anxious. She may be unable to sleep, and pace and/or bark ceaselessly. Report any of these changes to your vet, so that he or she can rule out any underlying medical problem before diagnosing CDS. As for Alzheimer's, there are some drug treatments now available to slow the deterioration and offer temporary improvement, but there is no cure. Proper nutrition and an appropriate exercise program may also help dogs with CDS.

The acronym DISH is frequently used to summarize the symptoms of CDS: it stands for disorientation, interaction changes, sleep (or activity) changes, and housetraining (specifically, loss of).

AT A GLANCE: COGNITIVE DYSFUNCTION SYNDROME

Symptoms	Diagnosis	Treatment(s)
Disorientation or confusion; loss of housebreaking; sleeplessness; restlessness; uncharacteristic aggression or anxiety	Thorough exam, to rule out underlying medical problem causing behavior changes	Drug treatment to improve memory; regular physical and mental exercise; nutritional therapy; reinforcement of training

Cushing's Disease

Cushing's disease (hyperadrenocorticism) is a disorder of the adrenal glands in which excessive adrenal hormones are produced. There are a number of potential causes: abnormal pituitary gland function (the most common cause, by far), an adrenal gland tumor, a side effect of cortisone therapy for another condition, or an overactive adrenal gland.

At a Glance: Cushing's Disease

Symptoms	Diagnosis	Treatment(s)
Increased appetite and drinking; increased urination; "pot belly"; hair loss	Urine and blood tests, X-rays, or ultrasound	Depending on cause: drug treatment, commonly mitotane; surgery to remove tumor, if present

The signs of Cushing's, a slowly progressing disease, often escape notice or are attributed to "just aging": increased appetite, increased drinking and urination, reduced activity, and development of a "pot belly." These symptoms typically worsen over time. Your dog may become obese, lose hair on both sides of her body (this may be the only obvious change), or pant heavily. Extensive laboratory tests and X-rays or ultrasound may be needed to diagnose the condition, find the cause, and plan treatment. The success of treatment depends in large part on the specific cause. If drug treatment is called for, your dog will have to be carefully monitored, as the drug is very strong: it destroys the adrenal gland tissue and decreases cortisol production. Your vet will need to ensure that only the right amount of the adrenal glandular tissue is being destroyed.

Cushing's is also fraught with complications, including skin and urinary tract infections—which must be treated with antibiotics—and diabetes mellitus and pancreatitis.

Dental Disease

Canine periodontal disease is the result of poor or absent dental care. It begins with plaque (formed when bacteria multiply on the teeth and gums), which when mixed over time with saliva, hardens to become tartar and calculus. These substances then irritate the gums, which turn red and tender, a stage called gingivitis. Left unchecked, the gums eventually begin to separate from the teeth, forming pockets for more bacteria and food particles. Finally, the bacteria attack the roots of the teeth and bone tissue in the jaw. Your dog now will probably be in pain; her gums may bleed; she'll have bad breath and trouble eating.

At a Glance: Periodontal Disease

Symptoms	Diagnosis	Treatment(s)
Bad breath and yellow, crusty teeth; trouble eating, especially dry, hard food; swollen, red, or bleeding gums; loose teeth	Full physical exam and medical history; exam of mouth, teeth, and gums; possibly blood and other diagnostic tests to evaluate status of major organs	Professional cleaning, with recommendations for regular dental home care; potential switch to tartar- or plaque-control dog food

Worse may be yet to come: if still left untreated, the bacteria may enter the bloodstream, a highway to the major organs, potentially infecting the heart, kidneys, lungs, and liver. Left unaddressed, periodontal disease–incited damage to your dog's major organs can cause death.

Small dogs, such as Pekingese and shih tzu, are at greater risk because their teeth are crowded into a much smaller mouth.

Conscientious dental care (see Chapter 5), at home and professionally, is the only way to prevent periodontal disease.

Diabetes Mellitus

Diabetes mellitus is caused by the failure of your dog's pancreas to produce enough insulin, the hormone that helps the body process blood sugar. Obesity is strongly implicated as a contributing factor to this incurable disease, so proper nutrition and exercise, as described in Chapter 5, are important preventive measures you can take.

Watch for increased water consumption—considerable—coupled with increased urination. Also, your dog may seem to be eating heartily and more often, yet still be losing weight.

At a Glance: Diabetes Mellitus

Symptoms	Diagnosis	Treatment(s)
Insatiable thirst, increased urination; weight loss though appetite has increased; eye cloudiness	Blood and urine tests	Primarily, insulin injections; medication to lower the blood glucose concentration; dietary management

Most dogs diagnosed with diabetes will require insulin injections, usually twice a day, although some can be maintained on once-daily injections. Close monitoring by your veterinarian will be necessary to ensure that the dose of insulin remains at the proper level to maintain optimal blood glucose concentration. If the dose is too low, serious illness usually results; if the dose is too high, it can cause seizures and death.

Having a Seizure

Though dogs of any age may experience seizures, older dogs are more prone to them. There are a number of possible causes: trauma or infection, low blood sugar, hypothyroidism, toxins in the blood, external poisons, or a tumor growing off the skull and pressing on the brain. Blood tests are usually run first to confirm or rule out various types of seizures; when a brain tumor is suspected, a CAT scan or MRI is usually recommended. These tumors often are operable if found early.

Seizure behavior is not the same in all cases. Some dogs will fall to the floor, writhing and foaming at the mouth, legs flailing in the air; others will assume a "slumping" posture—head down and tail between legs—and whimper or howl. Often the eyes will bulge and the dog will bite her tongue.

If your dog has a seizure, take her to a vet as soon as it is over.

Effective diets for diabetes are now widely available, but do not implement any nutritional changes without the go-ahead from your vet. In many cases, you'll be given a prescription diet available only from a vet's office. And, typically, you'll be required to feed your dog twice daily to coordinate with the insulin injections.

Eye Diseases

You may have noticed that your old dog, though still bushy-tailed, is no longer bright-eyed. Aging dogs fall prey to a number of eye conditions, some more serious than others. As explained in Chapter 3, just like humans they are susceptible, in particular, to glaucoma and cataracts.

GLAUCOMA

Glaucoma is increased pressure within the eye, caused when the clear fluid that maintains the shape of the eye and nourishes the eye tissues can no longer drain properly. This in turn causes the eye to stretch and enlarge.

Glaucoma is classified as primary or secondary:

- Primary glaucoma is an inherited condition that usually begins in one eye, but almost always spreads to the other, leading to complete blindness. Primary glaucoma is prevalent in certain breeds, including American cocker spaniels, basset hounds, Chow Chows, Shar-Peis, Labrador retrievers, huskies, and elkhounds.
- Secondary glaucoma is caused by another eye disease, such as inflammation inside the eye, advanced cataracts (see below), cancer in the eye, or chronic retinal detachment.

At a Glance: Glaucoma

Symptoms	Diagnosis	Treatment(s)
Redness around the rim; bloodshot eyes; also, listlessness, decreased appetite; irritability	Pressure tests; other tests to determine underlying cause	Early stage—eye drops or drugs; later, surgery

Determining which eye disorder your pet has will determine the treatment needed and the prognosis. Your vet will measure the pressure in your dog's eyes (just as your eye doctor does for you), as well as perform other tests to check for underlying causes.

It's important to note that glaucoma in pets is more painful than glaucoma in humans, but this may not be apparent to you, as the signs may mimic those of many other problems: lethargy, decreased appetite, irritability, and so on. What you can watch for are red or bloodshot eyes and/or cloudy cornea.

Treatment depends on stage at time of diagnosis. When only one eye is affected, drug therapies in the form of eye drops (expensive) and pills help decrease fluid production or increase fluid drainage from the eye. However, these are used primarily to help prevent or delay the spread of the disease to the remaining visual eye. Ultimately, surgery is required, but usually only when there is still hope of restoring vision. Permanently blind eyes may be removed (and may be replaced with a prosthetic ball implant).

Cataracts

A cataract, an opacity or cloudiness in the lens of the eye, may have many causes. It may be congenital, age-related, disease-related (in particular, diabetes, in which case the development of cataracts is almost unavoidable), or due to trauma or dietary deficiency. The dog with cataracts is unable to see through the cloudy part of the lens, and if the entire lens is involved, the dog will be blind in that eye, or completely blind when both eyes are affected.

At a Glance: Cataracts

Symptoms	Diagnosis	Treatment(s)
Corneal cloudiness; if advanced, apparent blindness	Eye exam; blood tests to check for underlying cause(s); possibly ultra-sound	Surgery or dissolution of the cataract; eye drops

The most common symptom apparent to owners is cloudiness of the eye. However, a much less serious condition, nuclear sclerosis, can be mistaken for cataracts. This is not a disease, but an age-related condition that does not cause blindness. Only a veterinary ophthalmologist can tell the difference, through an eye exam.

The standard cataract treatment is surgical removal or dissolution of the cataract, but this is not recommended (it is invasive and expensive) unless your dog is in good health otherwise, she has cataracts in both eyes, and there is hope of restoring vision. (If your dog has vision in one eye, surgery is not recommended.) Following surgery, you will have to administer eye drops.

OTHER EYE CONDITIONS

In addition to the aforementioned nuclear sclerosis, your dog may also develop conjunctivitis ("pink eye"), an inflammation that has many potential causes: irritation or abrasion from shampoo, dust, or other foreign particles; allergies; and others. If your dog has conjunctivitis, you may see her pawing at her eye, and there will be redness and maybe discharge. After attempting to isolate the cause (not always possible), your vet may prescribe an eye ointment, an antibiotic or a corticosteroid (or both), to clear up infection and reduce irritation.

Aging dogs also commonly develop what's called, simply, dry eye—when the eye fails to produce enough tears to moisten and bathe the eye. In addition to age, allergies may be the cause; or it may occur as a side effect of medication your dog is taking. Redness

Special Treatment

Many veterinarians today limit the scope of their practice to one discipline, such as surgery or oncology (the study of tumors). That means you have access to highly trained experts in many fields, from cardiology, ophthalmology, dermatology, anesthesiology, nutrition, acupuncture, and many others.

According to the AVMA, a veterinary specialist is a graduate veterinarian who has successfully completed the process of board certification in an AVMA-recognized veterinary specialty organization. This requires extensive postgraduate training and experience, a credential review, and examinations set by the given specialty organization.

---

and discharge make dry eye fairly obvious. Treatment is usually in the form of an eye ointment, to increase tear production, or artificial tears. (Note: *Never* give your dog over-the-counter human versions of these products.) You'll also help to make your dog more comfortable by keeping her hair trimmed around the eyes and by cleaning the eye area regularly, with gauze or a cotton ball saturated with warm water.

Gastric Dilatation and Volvulus, or "Bloat"

Humans often complain of feeling bloated. It's certainly uncomfortable, but usually, it's not serious—we ate too much or ate foods that disagreed with us. But bloat in dogs is something else entirely: it is considered a life-threatening emergency, one of the most serious a dog may experience. Gastric dilatation and volvulus, nicknamed "bloat," occurs when the dog's normal digestion process fails to work properly. Trapped gas and/or food stretches the stomach many times its normal size, resulting in a bloated stomach (dilatation) and causing tremendous abdominal pain. For reasons still unclear to practitioners, the stomach then has a tendency to rotate (volvulus),

Note

Bloating is *not always* evident, so your awareness of the other symptoms is imperative.

twisting off its own blood supply and the exit routes for the gas inside. At this point, your dog's life is in danger—she could die in a matter of hours, in desperate pain, unless treated immediately.

If you see your dog drooling, retching, or attempting but unable to vomit, or acting restless—pacing and whining, for example—or you notice a sudden and rapid expansion of her stomach, heavy or rapid panting, or shallow breathing, get her to a veterinary hospital or emergency facility as quickly as you can. Do not stop to call the vet; do not do anything except get your dog to professional help, on the double. The earlier the veterinarian gets started with treatment, the better her chances for survival. Do not try to relieve the gas from the stomach and do not give her anything by mouth.

At a Glance: Bloat

Symptoms	Diagnosis	Treatment(s)
Drooling, retching, and attempts to vomit; distended stomach, occurring suddenly; anxiousness, restlessness, pacing; depression; weakness; shock	Physical exam; possible X-rays to determine if the stomach has rotated	For shock, intravenous fluids; to release the trapped gas, insertion of tube in stomach; possibly surgery to resituate the stomach properly

It is not known why bloat occurs, or why it occurs in certain dogs, but some preventive measures have been identified as possibly helpful:

- Feed your dog two or three meals a day instead of only one large meal.
- Don't let her exercise for at least an hour after she eats.
- Don't let her "wolf" her food.
- Keep water available at all times.

At greater risk are older dogs, male dogs, thin or overweight dogs, dogs with a fearful or anxious temperament, and breeds described as "deep-chested" (the chest from backbone to sternum is relatively long, and width is narrow. These include Afghan hounds, Airedale terriers, Akitas, Alaskan malamutes, Great Danes, greyhounds, and the setter breeds.) That said, small dogs are not immune to bloat.

Fortunately, bloat is not as deadly as it once was; today the survival rate is better than 80 percent, but it all depends on your quick recognition and quick action.

Heart Disease

A leading killer of dogs, heart disease can be either present at birth or acquired. The latter is far more common in older dogs. Two types of heart disease are most prevalent:

Arrhythmia

An irregular heartbeat (too fast or too slow) may accompany any heart disease. This is called arrhythmia, which can lead to sudden death. Depending on the cause, a number of medications are available to treat arrhythmia; pacemakers can also be implanted, but this is an expensive option (usually $1,000-plus).

- Chronic valvular heart disease (CVD): The heart valves fail to close properly, causing abnormal blood flow.
- Chronic obstructive pulmonary disease (COPD): The walls of the heart thin and weaken.

Both result in heart failure over time, when the heart can no longer pump at the rate necessary to meet the body's needs. As the heart tries harder to do its job, the damage worsens.

AT A GLANCE: HEART DISEASE

Symptoms	Diagnosis	Treatment(s)
None at early stages. Later: coughing, difficulty breathing; weakness and lethargy. Late stage: difficulty breathing even at rest; loss of appetite and corresponding weight loss; extreme weakness; fainting	Thorough physical exam; blood and urine tests; X-rays; electrocardiogram (EKG)	Drug treatments: typically, a diuretic (to reduce fluid buildup), heart strengthener, or vasodilator (to ease blood pumping); also, diet, in particular a low-salt diet

Early detection of heart disease is only possible through regular checkups, as generally there are no symptoms in the early stages of heart disease. Later, your dog will have difficulty breathing and develop a nagging cough. Diagnosis is first through a physical exam, to check heart rate and for unusual heart sounds, followed by chest

X-rays and an electrocardiogram (EKG) to record the heart's electrical activity.

HEARTWORM DISEASE

Heartworm disease, though it affects the heart, is different from other forms of canine heart disease in that its cause is external: mosquitoes transmit the larvae of the heartworm parasite to your dog.

AT A GLANCE: HEARTWORM

Symptoms	Diagnosis	Treatment(s)
Coughing; weakness; inability to exercise; nosebleed	Physical exam, blood tests, X-rays; for final diagnosis, heartworm antigen test	Drug regimen

Once the larvae penetrate your dog's skin and invade the tissues, they continue to grow bigger as they migrate. After they take up lodging in your dog's heart, these worms can grow as long as fourteen inches. Left untreated, they can cause death.

Prevention of the disease is through an annual heartworm test and preventive drug treatment. If your dog is thought to have heartworm disease, she will have a complete workup, including chest X-rays and blood tests. The diagnosis usually is confirmed through the use of a heartworm antigen (a substance that evokes an immune response) test.

Treatment involves prescription medications called adulticides, which commonly are derivatives of arsenic.

Hip Dysplasia

Hip dysplasia is an inherited disease common in many large breeds; it develops when a dog is still a pup, though many dogs won't show symptoms until their geriatric years. In addition to genetic predisposition, lack of exercise is implicated in the development of the disease because exercise helps to maintain muscle mass around the hip joints, giving them greater stability.

AT A GLANCE: HIP DYSPLASIA

Symptoms	Diagnosis	Treatment(s)
Lameness in hind legs; change in gait; expression of pain on getting up/down and stretching limbs	X-rays of hip	Nonsteroidal anti-inflammatory drugs (NSAIDs); neutraceuticals, such as glucosamine and chondroitin sulfate; surgery

Signs of hip dysplasia are easy to spot. You'll notice your dog seems stiff and sore in the area of her back legs; she may start to walk "funny"; and you may hear her whimper or cry out when she gets up and down or stretches her back legs. Mild symptoms can be successfully controlled through drugs known collectively as nonsteroidal anti-inflammatory drugs (NSAIDs), common among them Rimadyl, Etogesic, and Deramaxx. These drugs are relatively safe, but monitoring of liver and kidney function is required, especially for long-term use. Neutraceuticals, typically glucosamine or chondroitin sulfate, are also prescribed.

For dogs whose discomfort cannot be relieved with drug or neutraceutical therapies, total hip replacement is the surgical treatment of choice, especially for those suffering from both hip dysplasia and moderate to severe arthritis. But the cost (in the thousands of dollars) may be prohibitive for many dog owners. Other less costly surgeries are also possible, to decrease pain.

Hypothyroidism

Hypothyroidism is a very common hormone imbalance found in older dogs, caused by the natural deficiency of the thyroid hormone. Certain breeds seem predisposed to develop hypothyroidism,

Bad Drug or Bad Press?

Recently, Rimadyl, a popular pain reliever for arthritis, hip dysplasia, and other mobility disorders, came under fire as a dangerous drug when it was implicated in the deaths of a number of pets. Pet owners spread the word fast over the Internet, warning against its use. Dr. Goldston contends that it is a safe and effective drug, but that its use must be monitored *carefully*, because in a small number of patients, severe liver damage and even death can occur. Unfortunately, this did not become widely known until several animals had died. Now, he says, problems can be avoided by periodic liver function testing (LFT), discontinuing use in those dogs whose LFTs are abnormal.

Other effective drug options are now available, but says Goldston, they all carry the same degree of risk as Rimadyl. If your vet prescribes any of these drugs for your pet, talk over concerns you may have *before* you begin treatment.

including: the Doberman pinscher, golden retriever, Irish setter, Great Dane, dachshund, and the boxer.

Deficiency of the thyroid hormone may be due to a number of reasons, but in the aging dog, most cases are due to natural atrophy of the gland or a congenital problem. Unfortunately, due to variations in the hormone level, testing and treatment are not that simple. Consequently, if your vet suspects hypothyroidism, he or she may recommend a drug protocol for several months and watch for improvement, as proof of diagnosis. Frequently, your dog will begin to feel peppier within the first week, although her hair probably will not begin to regrow for as long as four months into the treatment.

AT A GLANCE: HYPOTHYROIDISM

Symptoms	Diagnosis	Treatment(s)
Skin abnormality or infection; hair loss, often around collar and tail; dry or brittle hair; obesity; listlessness; anemia	Begin treatment to verify diagnosis	Drug treatment

Incontinence

Incontinence, the inability to control urination *or* defecation voluntarily, is not a disease, but it is linked to so many aging-dog illnesses and conditions that is deserves to be included in this listing.

Among the many problems that may contribute to incontinence are:

Dog diapers are gender-specific

- Kidney disease (chronic renal failure), Cushing's disease, diabetes, and urinary tract infections all are implicated in incontinence.
- If your dog is taking steroids, she may drink more water and need to urinate more often.
- If your dog has orthopedic pain, it may hurt for her to squat; or if your dog has mobility problems, she may have trouble getting in and out of the door, especially where steps are involved.
- Aging bladder and bowel muscles may cause her to lose control.
- Onset of "doggie Alzheimer's," cognitive dysfunction syndrome (CDS), can cause your dog to forget all her housebreaking training.

Many owners have difficulty treating incontinence in an aging dog. In addition to the obvious problem of cleanup, pet owners often struggle with feelings of anger and impatience. And because they know the dog can't help "having accidents," they then feel guilty for scolding the dog or becoming frustrated.

Depending on the cause of incontinence in your dog, in some cases it can be alleviated, for example by adjusting medication levels (only your vet should do this). In other cases, it will require adjustments on your part. You will need to be more vigilant and will probably have to walk her or let her out more often. If she is incontinent in her sleep, you can "wet-proof" the bed, as you would for a human infant: place a layer of plastic over her bed, then cover it with easy-to-wash towels or other comfy fabric. Another option is to use doggie diapers, which are available through many pet supply stores and catalogs, like the one shown here from Drs. Foster & Smith. But to avoid skin irritation, you will have to change these diapers just as you would for a child, and keep the diaper area clean (it will help to clip her hair short in this area). Ask your vet about dog-friendly versions of diaper rash ointments and baby wipes.

If the cause of your dog's accidents is related to CDS, it might help to do some retraining—housebreak her as you would a puppy, praising for a job well done.

Kidney Disease (Chronic Renal Failure)

As a dog ages, her kidneys may begin to function less efficiently, failing to filter the waste products and toxins from the blood and into the bladder, for release in urine. Instead, these toxins circulate to the kidneys and build up in the blood. (Note: A second kind of kidney failure, called acute kidney failure, is usually caused when a dog has ingested poison, such as antifreeze, or experiences other trauma. This can happen to dogs of any age, whereas aging dogs are particularly susceptible to chronic kidney disease.)

Though there is no cure for chronic kidney disease, it can be managed, long term in some cases, depending on its stage at the time of diagnosis. Unfortunately, sometimes as much as two-thirds

At a Glance: Kidney Disease

Symptoms	Diagnosis	Treatment(s)
Increased thirst and excessive urination; loss of housebreaking; lethargy or weakness	Blood and urine tests; possibly X-rays or ultrasound of the kidneys	Low-salt, low-protein (or hydrolyzed protein) diet, often by prescription only; subcutaneous fluid injections; additional dietary supplements

of kidney function may be lost before the disease is caught, making early diagnosis key. To that end, vets often begin to test for kidney failure as part of the senior dog wellness exam. For your part, be on the lookout for increased thirst and urination in your dog. She may have to urinate so often that she begins to have accidents. If this is happening with your dog, take her in to see your vet as soon as possible.

Liver Disease

As the largest gland in the body, and serving so many complex functions, the liver is subject to damage from a number of diseases. As individual cells in the liver become damaged by disease, the organ's ability to function decreases. If the disease is left unchecked, liver failure may result. But, miraculously, the liver can regenerate, so if caught early enough and treated properly, a dog diagnosed with liver disease can recover.

At a Glance: Liver Disease

Symptoms	Diagnosis	Treatment(s)
Loss of appetite, hence weight; listlessness; jaundice; increased thirst; dark urine; fluid buildup in the abdomen; pale gums	Palpation of abdomen; exam of eyes and gums for jaundice; bloodwork; possibly, a liver biopsy	Nutritional therapy; antibiotics, in the presence of infection

In older dogs, the signs of liver disease—which may appear quickly or slowly—include loss of appetite, followed by weight loss; listlessness; jaundice; increased thirst; dark urine; fluid buildup in the abdomen (which you may mistake for the onset of obesity); and pale or yellow gums.

Because the liver can be the site of so many diseases, understandably there are also many possible causes, which can only be determined by a thorough exam by your vet, including blood tests and, possibly, a biopsy. It follows, then, that there is more than one treatment, based on the cause and the level of damage when diagnosed. That said, nutritional therapy is often the treatment of choice for liver disease, to provide the proper quantities and types of proteins, carbohydrates, fats, and vitamins.

Reproductive Organ Conditions

Though dogs suffer different problems based on their gender, the prevention and cure for such health concerns revolve around a single solution: spaying and neutering. It can't be said often enough: dogs can benefit from spaying/neutering *at any age*.

PYOMETRA

Simply, pyometra, an infection of the uterus, can be fatal to an older, unspayed dog. This infection has two varieties. In the more common form, *open pyometra*, the cervix is open, and a smelly vaginal discharge is the most obvious sign. In the second variety, *closed pyometra*, there is no vaginal discharge, making diagnosis more difficult. Of the two, the closed version is usually more serious, since dogs become toxic from the unreleased urine contents.

Early on, before any discharge is apparent, the signs of pyometra mimic those of many other ailments, including poor appetite, vomiting, and increased thirst. Once diagnosed via lab work and possibly X-rays and ultrasound, typically your dog's uterus and ovaries

At a Glance: Pyometra

Symptoms	Diagnosis	Treatment(s)
Loss of appetite; increased thirst; vaginal discharge; vomiting	Blood tests; X-rays; ultrasound	Surgery; antibiotics

will be surgically removed. Don't mistake this for routine spaying, however, because once your dog has this potentially deadly infection, the risks accompanying this surgery rise exponentially—along with the price.

Prostate Problems

Unneutered dogs run a high risk of developing one form or an-other of prostatic disease, which include infections, enlargement, abscesses, and cancer.

At a Glance: Prostate Problems

Symptoms	Diagnosis	Treatment(s)
Loss of appetite; sensitivity to touch on abdomen; constipation; pain during urination; cloudy or bloody urine; hunched appearance	Blood tests; X-rays; ultrasound	Surgery; antibiotics

Other Concerns

Other common health concerns of elderly dogs include:

- *Anemia.* The blood is deficient in red blood cells, in hemoglobin, or in total volume. Anemia may be associated with kidney disease, cancer, and other illnesses. It can cause extreme weakness and, without treatment, may become so severe that emergency medical help will be required.

- *Bladder tumors.* These are the most common tumors of the urinary tract. Early diagnosis (via X-rays, urinalysis, aspiration, biopsy, and other means) is imperative for effective treatment (though a cure is rare), which includes surgery, chemotherapy, and/or radiation.
- *Degenerative myelopathy (DM).* This is a progressive disease of the spinal cord, leading to respiratory failure and paralysis. It is thought to be an autoimmune dysfunction. The signs of DM include incontinence, loss of coordination/stability in the legs, weakness, and shakiness. Sadly, the diagnosis for DM can only be confirmed after death, and there is no treatment—though exercise, swimming in particular, may slow its progress.

SUMMARY

It's inevitable: your old friend one day will get sick. You know that, but somehow it never makes the bad news easier to accept when it comes. And before you even have a chance to deal with your own feelings, you must begin to cope with the practicalities. Your vet will explain what's wrong with your dog, of course, and give detailed treatment and care options and requirements. But it will be up to you to decide how you will proceed; to consider how much you can handle practically and financially; and, ultimately, to determine what is best for your dog. The more you know in advance, the better you'll understand what you are facing when the time comes, and the better equipped you'll be to make informed decisions, so that you can chart the right course for you and your dog.

KEY PET POINTS

- Make sure you thoroughly understand your dog's diagnosis, prognosis, and treatment options. It's a good idea to ask your vet to write down this information, so that you can review it carefully at home and to have on hand should you decide to consult a specialist.

- Many types of treatments, both traditional and alternative, are now options for many age-related canine conditions. Keep your mind open to the possibilities.
- Be honest with yourself and with your vet when it comes to designing a treatment plan for your dog. If you are squeamish when it comes to handling needles, for example, or cleaning wounds, be up front about it so that both you and your dog can get the help you need.

CHAPTER 7

Dollar Signs: Managing the Costs of Senior Pet Care

Finance managers often conduct cost-benefit analyses to determine whether the benefit of doing something is worth the money it takes to do it. No such cut-and-dry method exists for evaluating the benefits versus the costs of caring for your aging dog. After all, you can't put a price tag on keeping your best friend alive and well and by your side for as long as possible. Still, money *is* a concern for many pet owners. All the advances made in veterinary medicine in the recent past come at a price, some of them very high—into the many thousands of dollars, in some cases. And that's not counting the cost of premium food, mobility aids, and whatever other supplies may be necessary to keep your dog comfortable and safe in his golden years. In the last five years, costs for veterinary services have risen 73 percent to $19 billion; and according to the American Pet Products Manufacturers Association (APPMA), Americans were expected to spend $35.9 billion on pet care in 2005.

Even though most pet owners report they "would do anything it takes to save their dog," that "anything" can translate to financial hardship. In worst-case scenarios, people may feel forced to give up their dogs (one of the main reasons given for turning pets in to shelters is cost of care); others who can't afford expensive medical care will have their dogs euthanized instead. How can you avoid going to such extremes?

You already know four of the best ways to keep the cost of care down for your aging dog:

1. Take your dog for twice-yearly checkups.
2. Feed your dog high-quality food.
3. Control your dog's weight.
4. Exercise and groom (including dental care) your dog regularly.

Together, these preventive measures are worth more than a pound of cure; they can add up to a ton of savings. In particular, when you take your dog in for regular checkups, your vet can detect internal disease processes before (sometimes long before) they exhibit external signs. As in human medicine, the earlier problems are detected and treated (or, ideally, prevented), the less expensive they will be over the long term.

Eventually, however, most owners of aging dogs will find themselves staring down at a bottom line with way too many digits. As you know by now, senior dogs—and especially those into their geriatric years—are much more likely to require high-price surgeries, daily meds, and other therapies. In fact, two-thirds of your dog's health problems will occur in the last one-third of his life. It will be tough enough coping practically and emotionally with the fading health of

Buyer Beware

The costs of your dog's veterinary care should be commensurate with the degree and depth of specialized care he is receiving. Never let price be your only criterion, or you may get what you pay for. For example, a clinic offering a low-cost spay/neuter operation may not administer IV fluids after surgery, provide post-op pain relief, or even use sterile surgery techniques. When you comparison shop, ask more than how much; ask for the details of procedures and policies as well.

your faithful companion; why not eliminate the worry about whether you'll be able to afford his care? Here are some guidelines for taking the bite out of the costs of caring for your senior dog:

- Think ahead.
- Take advantage of cost-saving programs.
- Avail yourself of other cost-cutting options.

THINK AHEAD

The best way to ensure you'll be able to cover the cost of your pet's care over the long term is to think about it well before you have to pull out your wallet.

Do Some Research

It will help to have some idea what veterinary costs might be over the life of your dog. This kind of information is readily available. Here are some places to start:

- Take a quick trip to the Web site of the American Society for the Prevention of Cruelty to Animals (ASPCA),www.aspca.org, where you'll find a clearly laid-out table of costs, by animal.

- While you're online, tap over to the American Kennel Club's Web site, www.akc.org; click first on "Future Dog Owners," then "About Buying a Dog," to get an overview of the cost implications of dog ownership. Also follow the "Be a Responsible Dog Owner" link, which categorizes a number of care issues, many with cost implications.

- If you have a purebred dog, you might also want to familiarize yourself with his breed's susceptibility to certain health disorders, which can help prepare you for possible veterinary costs down the road. A good place to do that is the online version of the *Merck Veterinary Manual,* which you'll find at: www.merck vetmanual.com/mvm/index.jsp. There you can search, for free, by topic, species, specialty, disease, and keyword.

Save for a Rainy Day

It's a familiar refrain, but one of the most effective ways of preparing yourself for the long-term care of your dog is to open a savings account for him—put money aside each month, for example, as you would for a child's education, so that the money will be there when you need it. This is a favorite recommendation among financial planners for their pet-owner clients.

Buy Health Insurance for Your Dog

Pet insurance has been around for a while now, but, currently, only a very small percentage of pet owners invest in it—around 5 percent (3 percent of dogs and 1 percent of cats are insured, according to the APPMA's National Pet Owner's Survey), up from just 1 percent approximately a decade ago. Pet insurance is likely to become an integral part of veterinary medicine as more pet owners take advantage of higher-cost services offered by veterinary specialists.

The considerations for pet insurance are pretty much the same as those for the human version: price of premiums, deductibles, exclusions for preexisting conditions, and so on. And, needless to say, older dogs are considered higher-risk, hence you'll pay more for coverage—if you can get it at all. So, investing in pet health insurance is best done before your dog is older and needs it. That said, if your senior dog is still healthy, health insurance may still be worth investigating.

Here are three companies that offer pet insurance:

Veterinary Pet Insurance (the oldest and best known)
Phone: 800-899-4VPI
Web site: www.pet.insurance.com

PetCare Pet Insurance
Phone: 866-275-PETS
Web site: www.petcarepals.com

Petshealth Care Plan
Phone: 800-807-6724
Web site: www.petshealthplan.com

Be diligent in your investigation of any pet insurance provider:

- Read the policies thoroughly—including the fine print, especially as it applies to older pets and preexisting conditions, premiums, co-pays, and annual caps.
- Call your state's insurance department to make sure any company you're considering doing business with is registered with state regulators. Not all companies are approved in all fifty states.
- If you go online to check out these companies, verify that all your questions are answered there. If you're not sure, call and request paper copies of the policies.
- Sit down with your calculator to figure out what these policies will cost over the predicted lifespan of your dog. Then, as accurately as possible, calculate what you've been spending out-of-pocket on pet care each year. Compare the numbers. Also

HOLLY'S STORY: GOT YA COVERED

The year we spent $10,000 on dog care was the year we learned how to spell "p-e-t i-n-s-u-r-a-n-c-e." At that time, several years ago, purchasing medical insurance for our older dogs, even without "preexisting conditions," was extremely expensive. While that has not changed much, types of care covered and reimbursements have changed significantly. And obtaining a policy when a dog is young is very affordable.

When we adopted two-year-old Holly, an auburn Cavalier King Charles spaniel, in 1999, we arranged for insurance through a pet insurance company with a long history and a great deal of experience in insuring pets, as well as an excellent reputation and a "menu" of coverage options. For Holly, we now have routine care coverage (vaccinations, heartworm protection, annual exams, routine blood tests, and more), "major medical" (unexpected illnesses, accidents, medical tests, surgeries, hospitalization, and cancer treatment), and a cancer rider that provides additional benefits for cancer treatment, for an annual premium of less than $500. Every year we've had the insurance, it has paid for itself many times over, most recently covering 70 percent of the costs of replacing a torn ligament in Holly's leg.

All our other adopted dogs, unfortunately, have been too old to be insured affordably, so we are always alert for other options to help with medical costs. One day as we waited for one of them to undergo an expensive diagnostic test, our veterinarian told us about a credit card for financing specific types of health care, including veterinary care. There are various repayment plans, including some that incur no interest charges if the

balance is paid within a specified time. We filled out an
application on the spot, our veterinarian's staff called
in the information, and we received approval while
we waited. We used the card that very day to pay for
the test, and it remains a resource for large expenses,
especially unanticipated ones.

—April Cormaci, New Jersey

consider potential "catastrophic" expenses: Would you be able
and/or willing to pay, for example, $6,000 to $10,000 if your
dog became seriously ill near the end of his life expectancy?
And be aware that, to date, most policies require you to pay for
your vet's services at time of treatment; you then file a claim
and wait for approval and reimbursement. However, HMO-
type programs are becoming more widely available. With this
type of policy, you don't pay up front; your vet submits the
paperwork to the insurance company to get paid.

The AVMA, which supports the concept of pet health insurance,
has identified a number of criteria that any pet health insurance
program should meet. It should:

1. Have the support of the veterinary community (veterinary
   associations, private practitioners).
2. Allow pet owners to choose their own veterinarian and to seek
   referrals of their choice.
3. Be in compliance with the policies of the insurance commis-
   sion of the state in which the policies are issued.
4. Give clear control to the veterinarian to monitor the health of
   the pet.

TAKE ADVANTAGE OF PROGRAMS

Unlike pet health insurance, which puts senior dogs at a disadvantage because of their age, you may be able to get some bottom-line relief in the form of cost-saving programs that actually put old dogs first in line.

Package Programs

To educate pet owners about all-important biannual exams for its "senior citizens," a number of veterinary practices across the country are offering cost-saving "package" care programs for their patients over seven years of age. Rather than charging individually for the standard components of the wellness exam (see Chapter 4), they're charging a flat rate for the entire workup, sometimes cutting the cost by as much as a third.

Awareness Programs

During various months in the year, to promote senior pet awareness programs, humane organizations, clinics, and even some private veterinary practices show their support by cutting costs during the month, either for overall care or just for the "featured" health issue. For example:

- Every November, the ASPCA celebrates Adopt-a-Senior-Pet Month nationwide; other local humane organizations have followed suit with similar programs (though not always at the same time), and many offer lower-cost senior care coverage to promote awareness.
- As noted in Chapter 5, the American Veterinary Medical Association, along with veterinary dental organizations, celebrates National Pet Dental Health Month, usually in February (see www.petdental.com). Find out where in your community "deals" may be offered for dental checkups and cleanings (your vet's office may be one of them).

Don't hesitate to nose around for others: ask your vet if he or she participates in any low- or reduced-cost care programs; call your local humane organization or veterinary hospital to find out whether they sponsor low- or reduced-cost clinics for yearly vaccinations; and check with other dog owners you know.

"Angel" Programs

If you are a low-income pet owner, you may be able to find financial assistance in the form of an "angel," an individual or an organization that helps qualified pet owners get their dogs the care they need when they can't afford it themselves.

Remember Frisky, from Chapter 3? His guardian angel helped defray the costs of his care throughout his life. And there are more out there like her. All the vets interviewed for this book were aware of such angels in their midst—though, understandably, these Good Samaritans do not "advertise," so you'll have to ask for help if you need it. Your vet is the best place to start; or call your local humane organization.

You can also do some research into organizational assistance programs. Humane organizations as well as professional veterinary associations typically sponsor these. Here are three, to give you some idea of the various forms of aid available:

- The Marin Humane Society (Marin County, California) sponsors a SHARE (Special Human-Animal Relationships) program, the largest part of which is its Side-by-Side program. Side-by-Side matches financial support, volunteer efforts, and donated services with qualified pet "guardians" in need. Depending on the situation, pet owners may receive pet food, veterinary care, grooming, regular visits by volunteers, transportation to the veterinarian or groomer, and much more. Side-by-Side is currently assisting some 220 pet owners with 150 dogs (as well as 196 cats and 38 birds). 415-883-4621; www.marinhumanesociety.org

- The American Animal Hospital Association (AAHA) launched its Helping Pets Fund in 2004 to help those in need get quality care for sick or injured pets. The AAHA fund offers aid for three types of cases: low-income individuals on government assistance; pet owners experiencing a financial hardship; and Good Samaritans who find an animal in need, whether abandoned or whose owner cannot afford to care for it. Note that this fund does not give money directly to individuals; an AAHA-accredited veterinary clinic must apply on behalf of them. 866-4HELPETS; www.aahahelpingpets.org
- Human senior citizens with senior pets may find help through the Pets for the Elderly Foundation (PEF), described in Chapter 4. 866-849-3598; www.petsfortheelderly.org

Wellness Programs

Another cost-saving option comes in the form of wellness programs, which offer comprehensive affordable health care services. For the price of enrollment, you can save as much as 50 percent on routine medical care for your pet, and typically are given the options to pay in advance or in low monthly payments. Two programs to check out are:

- Banfield Optimum Wellness Plans, offered through nearly four hundred PetSmart superstores across the country. Read more about them at www.petsmart.com/banfield or call PetSmart at 623-580-6100.
- Pet Assure, a pet care saving program, offers a 25 percent discount every time you visit one of its 2,500 participating vets. (Note: Some companies now offer this program as an employee benefit. Check with your human resources department. If they don't offer it now, they might consider it. Employers can call 888-789-PETS, or e-mail employeebenefits@petassure.com to learn more.) To find a Pet Assure provider in your area, go to www.petassure.com.

AVAIL YOURSELF OF OTHER OPTIONS

Three other options you might want to consider for helping you manage your dog's care costs are:

- *Comparison shop for medications and supplements.* Purchasing medications directly from your vet is almost always much more expensive than if you purchase them from a pet supply catalog, an online pharmacy, a compounding pharmacy (which custom pre-pares meds), or even from your own pharmacy. Though you will still need a written or phoned-in prescription from your vet, with this in hand, you can access numerous cost-effective alternative sources for your dog's medications. Here are three places to start:

Safety First

Though your goal in comparison shopping for medications is to save money, price should *not* be your primary criterion: safety should. Especially if you prefer to shop on the Web, you must take the precaution of checking out any online pharmacy before you buy— your dog's life may depend on it, as well as your own security. Red flags to watch for: if the pharmacy does not require a prescription from your vet, go elsewhere; if the pharmacy requests personal information from you, such as your SSN, back out of there. Due diligence in this regard is easy enough to do. Either call the National Association of Boards of Pharmacy (NABP), at 847-698-6227, or go to its Web site, www.nabp.net, to find out if the pharmacy you're considering doing business with is licensed and in good standing.

The best advice is to get a recommendation from someone you know and trust. Generally, even your vet will be happy to steer you to cheaper sources to ensure your dog gets the treatment he needs.

Internet Pets: www.internetpets.com
Drs. Foster & Smith: www.drsfostersmith.com
Pet Med Express: www.1800PetMeds.com

- *Get a second opinion on expensive procedures and treatments.* This is just common sense. You'd do it for yourself or another member of your human family before undergoing major surgery, for example, and it's the best practice where your dog is concerned, too.
- *Consider credit.* Going into debt is never a good idea, but in dire straits, it may be your only option. If you find yourself in this position and your dog needs treatment *now*, check out CareCredit, a health care payment plan that offers several payment options, one of which is interest-free as long as you can pay at least the minimum monthly payment. Learn more about CareCredit at http://carecredit.com, or call 800-859-9975. You may also be able to work out a payment plan with your veterinarian, especially if you have a longstanding relationship and have always paid your bills on time.
- *Contact your local animal shelter.* They may operate or know of a local subsidized veterinary clinic or assistance program.

SUMMARY

Our dogs are worth their weight in gold to us, and we can't imagine anything we wouldn't do for them. But then comes the day we have to imagine exactly that: we have to somehow put an actual

---

One-Stop Shopping

Online shoppers for pet supplies and services of all kinds should go to www.bhejei.com/mailorder.htm, which has lengthy lists of sources in all categories of pet care.

dollar figure on our love and care. It's never easy to do, but by taking the shock value out of the equation, you'll have an easier time of it. Remember, two-thirds of your dog's health problems will occur in the last one-third of his life. Enjoy the first two-thirds of your dog's years with you for all they're worth, but prepare yourself for the last third. Money may be a concern, but it doesn't have to be an obstacle to caring for your senior dog. Be proactive: do some research and explore all options.

KEY PET POINTS

- Start today, if you haven't already, implementing the preventive measures discussed throughout this book (biannual exams, proper nutrition, exercise, and grooming). Besides being the most conscientious way to care for your aging dog, doing so is the most effective way to save money on long-term veterinary care.
- If your dog is healthy and still on the young side of old, look into health insurance for him; or open a savings account in his name, so that you'll have the money you need when you need it for major health problems.
- Don't despair if you realize your budget will crack or break under the strain of paying for your dog's just-diagnosed major illness. Help is out there, in the form of programs, financial assistance, and credit plans.

PART 3

Quality-of-Life
and End-of-Life Issues

CHAPTER 8

Quality of Life: Answering the Hard Questions

Quality of life is a subjective, personal concept. Though sociologists, economists, and politicians talk about it as a quantifiable measure, usually applying the term to large groups of people for the purpose of defining behavior, establishing economic parameters, or setting public policy, no one can really say what constitutes quality of life for another. Sometimes we even have difficulty expressing for ourselves what it means, especially since it changes over time. So how can we be expected to do that for another species? Nevertheless, that's exactly what we are called upon to do: determine quality of life for our dogs, as they near the end of their lifespan. As the guardians of our pets' well-being, we must somehow decide whether their lives are still worth living.

As close as we are to our dogs, as much as we understand them and they us, it is at this point that we run up against the familiar communication problem. When our dogs become ill, they cannot tell us in so many words what is wrong, "where it hurts," nor can they tell us whether they still take pleasure in living or that the pain or discomfort they're experiencing is too much to bear.

But we're not flying totally blind here. Just as when they first became ill and gave us signs we learned to recognize, as their disease or illness progresses, dogs give quality-of-life clues, too, clues we need to pick up on to ensure that these final days we spend with them bring their own kind of joy, borne of respect for a life well lived and respect for a peaceful closure to that life. It is by asking, and attempting to answer, quality-of-life questions that those clues reveal themselves:

- What constitutes quality of life for a dog?
- How can I tell when my dog is in pain or discomfort? If so, can my dog's pain be managed, and for how long?
- How much longer does my dog have to live? How will I know when it is time to "let go"?

WHAT CONSTITUTES QUALITY OF LIFE FOR MY DOG?

Dogs may not be great communicators when it comes to expressing sickness or discomfort, but they leave no doubt in anyone's mind when they're consumed with joy, and joy, by anyone's definition, is a sure sign of quality of life. Conversely, the absence of joy, or pleasure, is a reliable benchmark that quality of life is on the wane. Of course, as your dog has aged and become ill or disabled, her displays of pleasure have become more subdued and short lived, but they're no less meaningful.

Vets agree on a number of criteria that constitute quality of life for an aging and/or sick dog, which can be presented as a series of questions you can ask to determine it for your own dog:

- Does she look forward to eating?
- Is she happy to see you when you come home—even if it takes her longer to find you and tell you so?
- Does she sleep comfortably? Or does she rest fitfully—pacing and/or staring throughout the night?

- Can she still enjoy exercise, even if just long enough to reach that sunny spot near the tree in the grass to loll in, and take an interest in the action around her?
- Is she able to urinate/defecate without difficulty? Or is she often incontinent, or strains when she tries to "go."
- Does she seem content, peaceful? Or does she vocalize—bark, whine—incessantly, and at nothing? Is she restless, unable to get comfortable—constantly getting up and down, "fluffing" her bedding?
- How about her temperament: Is she still sweet and loving, or has she become snappish and irritable?

Remember the guideline in Chapter 2 on prevention, to trust your instincts? When it comes to sorting through quality-of-life criteria, you must give your instincts, your "hunches," your full attention. If you "just have a feeling" something's wrong, don't push it aside; follow it up. Your vet can help in this regard, to weigh the importance of signs from your dog and perceptions from you. He or she has expert knowledge of your dog's health status and, ideally, a great deal of insight into your feelings about the kind and level of care you want and can provide for your dog. That, coupled with your day-to-day experience with your dog, will help you answer whether your dog still has "quality of life."

CASEY'S STORY: QUALITY CARE, QUALITY LIFE

It was April 1993, and my husband and I were in Paris. Perhaps it was watching so many Parisians strolling along the streets with their dogs that made us decide it was time to adopt one of our own. When we returned to the States, we visited a nearby shelter, where initially we considered a young, eminently adoptable, cocker spaniel named Oliver—we decided he didn't "need us." We were more intrigued by a four-year-old we were told had been there about a month and wasn't adoptable. We asked to see him anyway, and soon found ourselves looking into the biggest brown eyes set in the sweetest of faces: this was the unadoptable Casey.

He *was* in a pretty miserable state. He had been scratching, chewing, and rubbing himself since being brought to the shelter, and had lost all the hair on his belly and his rear end. He had scabs, lesions, and hot spots all over. The staff had so far been unable to help him. We knew he was the one for us.

Ignoring protestations from the shelter staff, we took him home that day and to our local vet the next. He diagnosed and treated Casey for sarcoptic mange, a skin disease caused by microscopic mites that burrow under the skin. After an injection to kill the mites and three weeks of dosing with pediatric Benadryl every four hours to help control the itching, the mites breathed their last. Eventually, Casey's hair filled in and he became recognizable as a dog.

Like all adopted dogs, Casey came with "issues" beyond his skin condition. Only four years old, he already seemed like an old soul, a little old man. He didn't seem to know how to play, and he had terrible separation anxiety that no amount of treatment or training could calm. He hated thunder and would shake violently and crawl into my husband's lap for comfort during a storm, and he wouldn't go out in the rain. He did, however, have a less serious side. He would carry toys around the house, sometimes mouthing them, sometimes tearing them apart. And he was always game for a good howl: if one of us got him started, he would howl and bay and almost yodel just for the fun of it. He liked to relax curled up on one of his dog beds and, at night, snuggled up against my husband or me in our bed.

Over the years, Casey was joined by two other adoptees. When he was six, we took in a cocker spaniel–golden retriever mix that had been in two foster homes and was on his way back to a shelter. Clancy, as we named him, was a sleek and sophisticated, amiable sort, whose presence seemed to dispel Casey's separation anxiety. And when Casey was nine, we adopted Holly, a two-year-old auburn King Charles Cavalier spaniel, also destined for the shelter. Holly's tail constantly wagged and her tongue was always seeking a face, a leg, or an arm to lick. She and Casey bonded immediately. She taught him how to play; and they would sleep together, one head on the other's back, or curled up next to each other, and groom each other for hours.

All the dogs had annual physicals and periodic other procedures (teeth

Casey, guarding his stuffed pig.

cleaning, X-rays, blood tests, etc.) as well as the recommended vaccinations and so on. But it was caring for Casey's many "issues" that taught us the most about how best to care for all the other canine companions we would have in our lives.

Within a couple of years after he came to live with us, Casey developed a wound on one paw, which he licked constantly. Resistant at first to treatment, our vet finally recommended we consult a canine dermatologist, who found that Casey had allergies. So for the next several years, my husband administered regular allergy shots, which Casey stoically endured in exchange for treats. This was our first experience in the world of canine medical specialists. It would not be the last. Casey was also prone to ear infections, not unusual for dogs with large, floppy ears. He eventually developed severe calcification in one ear. A surgeon recommended sewing his ear closed, a common approach, but one that impairs hearing, and Casey was already losing his hearing. We returned to our regular vet for a second opinion. He recommended a less drastic approach, a Zepp procedure, which involves cutting a notch in the bottom of the ear opening to provide more access for air circulation. This simple less traumatic operation worked.

Next, we noticed him limping suddenly one day. It turned out to be the result of a torn ligament in his "knee" (a joint of his hind leg), a common injury for dogs that can occur simply by jumping and landing incorrectly. The ligament was replaced surgically by a piece of nylon, and he recovered full use of his leg in record time. Casey also developed glaucoma as he aged, which was monitored and treated by a wonderful ophthalmologist. Then the lens in one eye began to detach and, as the ophthalmologist had warned us, the day came when he suddenly began to squint, the sign of final detachment and pain. Surgery was needed to remove the lens. Though this resulted in less near vision, it apparently improved his far vision, and Casey seemed like a new dog for several years after.

—*April Cormaci, New Jersey*

Read the conclusion of Casey's story in the next chapter.

Dr. Richard Goldston says, "I usually advise owners that when they see their pet doing virtually none of the things that used to bring them happiness (such as barking when a loved one comes home, wanting to lie in the sun, etc.), then at that time I believe we are only prolonging dying, not prolonging meaningful living." Of course, he adds, that assumes your dog is getting proper veterinary care and that there are no other options available to offer a significant chance of improvement.

IS MY DOG IN PAIN?

For many pet owners, this is the first question they want answered when they learn their dog is ill—no one can stand the thought of a loved one suffering. For a long time, scientists debated whether animals *could* feel pain. Seems ridiculous, in retrospect, especially since it is now recognized that humans and animals experience pain in much the same way (our nervous systems are very similar). But there's still controversy over how animals actually experience physical pain and demonstrate it, thus how we can recognize it. No one questions, however, that pain is an important quality-of-life determinant.

For us, as caregivers, we need to address pain in two steps:

1. Identify pain.
2. Manage pain.

Identifying Pain

The American Animal Hospital Association (AAHA), in its 2005 "Senior Care Guidelines for Dogs and Cats," says, "Any behavioral change or change in vital signs may be an indication of pain." But that statement must be qualified, for as the AAHA points out, signs of pain may be affected by other factors, such as medications your dog is taking, or even your dog's demeanor (just like people, some dogs feel pain more intensely than others, and some "complain" of it more or less, too). To help pet owners and veterinarians recognize a dog in pain, Pfizer Inc.'s Animal Health division has identified "pain behaviors," in five categories (adapted and reprinted here with permission of Pfizer Animal Health, www.pfizerah.com):

Posture
- Tail between legs
- Arched or hunched back
- Twisted body, to protect pain site
- Drooped head
- Prolonged sitting position
- Tucked abdomen
- Lying in flat, extended position

Temperament
- Aggressive
- Clawing
- Attacking, biting
- Escaping

Vocalization
- Barking (excessive)
- Howling
- Moaning
- Whimpering

Locomotion
- Reluctance to move
- Carrying one leg
- Lameness
- Unusual gait
- Unable to walk

Other
- Unable to perform normal tasks
- Attacks other animals or people if painful site is touched
- Chewing painful areas (self-trauma)
- No interest in food or play

What about emotional pain? Do dogs feel it? Most dog owners and veterinary practitioners would say absolutely. Some scientists beg to differ. They believe only primates and humans have this capability. Other research, however, has shown that dogs (as well as cats, monkeys, and birds) demonstrate emotional distress in the form of behaviors, such as lack of motivation, separation anxiety, obsessive-compulsive disorder (OCD), unresponsiveness, loss of appetite, and others. Distress of this nature can intensify physical pain.

Managing Pain

Advances in veterinary medicine include a better, more thorough understanding of how animals feel and demonstrate pain. Pain

Go to the Videotape

To help pet owners better understand how animals experience pain, the International Veterinary Academy of Pain Management (IVAPM), at Colorado State University College of Veterinary Medicine, has prepared an insightful video titled "Is Your Pet in Pain?" It's viewable for free online at www.cvmbs.colostate.edu/ivapm.

management is now taught as part of the curriculum at many veterinary schools and as part of continuing education programs. There's even a Companion Animal Pain Management Consortium, formed to educate veterinary professionals and students alike on how to recognize and treat pain in pets. The result is that, today, numerous drug treatment options are available for treating pain in animals. Vets treat pain in advance, too—for example, before a major surgery.

Depending on the type of pain, whether *acute* (sudden onset and usually sharp and severe) or *chronic* (of long duration or frequent recurrence), single drugs or drug combinations may be used. Numerous drug types are available, including NSAIDs, opiate derivatives, antidepressants, anticonvulsants, local anesthetics, and numerous others. Drug modalities (methods) expand the possibilities for pain management still further. They include:

- Oral
- Injectable
- Transdermal (absorption through the skin)
- Transmucosal (absorption through a mucus membrane)

Pain management isn't all about drugs, either. The AAHA points out that, in combination with or as an alternative to drugs, relief may also be feasible in the form of:

- Acupuncture
- Physical therapy and massage
- Local and regional anesthesia
- Weight management (when appropriate)
- Environmental modification (bedding changes, access aids such as ramps, steps, and lifting products)

It would seem, then, that there's a pain treatment option for every dog and every condition. But pain management is complicated by the fact that the experience of pain is highly individual: the same cause of physical pain can have a wide variety of responses in different dogs. For example, one dog with arthritis in her back leg may limp or whine, giving clear indications of discomfort; another might simply slow down, which an owner might understandably mistake as just a sign of aging. Moreover, response to treatment can vary widely, as well.

Alleviating your pet's pain is essential not just because you don't want to see her suffer, but because pain can actually impede the healing process and cause other problems. Just the stress alone caused by pain can lower your dog's immune system, for example. For all these reasons, it's important that you and your vet work closely together to monitor both your dog's pain and her response and reactions to any prescribed pain protocol.

Probably the most effective way to monitor your pet's status is to use the log system described earlier in the book. On a calendar, note each day:

- Medications or other treatment your pet receives, including exact amounts, as well as her responses/reactions

- Food and water intake
- Behavior shifts
- Changes in her urine and stool, or problems relieving herself

One more thing: it's about you, too. All medicine goes down better when administered with love and patience. How you address your dog's pain and handle the treatment process will affect how well she responds. If you're tense and frightened, she will pick up on it; if you're frustrated and impatient, you'll probably be met with resistance. If, on the other hand, you take your time, to give both of you confidence in what you're doing, you will be able to add these moments of tender loving care to your long list of joyful memories shared with your dog. Don't hesitate to ask for help if you're having difficulty facing your pet's pain, disability, or physical impairment; administering medications; or just coping in general. If, for example, you start to find more of your dog's pills turning up in corners and behind furniture, signaling that she's found a way to outsmart you, return to your vet or veterinary technician for a retraining session; or ask if the medication is available in liquid form, which may be easier for you to administer. Think options and solutions: usually you'll find them.

HOW WILL I KNOW WHEN TO "LET GO"?

Thanks to the tremendous progress in veterinary medicine in the past few decades, our dogs are living longer lives of quality, sometimes even in the face of serious disease and illness. Not too long ago, many age-related ailments now being handled routinely could only have resulted in euthanasia.

But these advances are not without their disadvantages. For one, they make it much more difficult for vets to answer questions all dog lovers have when confronted with the end of their dog's life: How much longer does my dog have to live? Will I know when it's time to cease treatment?

It's About You, Too

Your dog's care may be imposing stress, a financial burden, a disruption to your daily life, or all of these. So you must consider your own state of mind at the same time you concern yourself with your dog's quality of life. The caregiver role is not an easy one, and it's all too easy to get lost in it—you're so busy taking care of the one who is sick that you get lost in the shuffle. For example, you come home from work to find your dog has been incontinent, or has vomited, all over your bedroom rug. After you clean that up, you make sure she is fed properly and gets her medications or treatment. You write down how much she ate and any other noteworthy comments about her health. Then you take her for a walk or spend time in the yard with her. When you come in, you spend time brushing her, because you know that kind of stimulation is good for an ailing dog—and what's more, she loves it. By now, you're too tired to make yourself dinner, so you have a quick snack or nibble on leftovers before heading to bed. But your dog is restless all night and keeps you awake with her pacing and demands to go outside. The next morning you're exhausted before your day even begins.

After weeks, or months, of that, you shouldn't be surprised if you're feeling overwhelmed, scared, even angry and frustrated, and just plain stressed-out. If you don't address those feelings, you'll do a disservice to both you and your dog, because your state of mind is an integral part of the level of care you're able to provide your dog. Ask yourself how your quality of life has changed, for better and for worse, since your animal began to require extra care:

1. Do you find yourself having conflicting emotions? For example, do you ever feel angry at the extra work it takes to care for your pet (perhaps you're living with an incontinent dog)? Do you then feel guilty for being angry? Do you also feel great joy and gratitude that you can share this time in your pet's life?

2. Do you feel you're learning valuable "life lessons" from the experience, or just learning how to get by on less sleep?
3. Do you find it easier to remember to take care of yourself because you must do so for your pet?
4. Have you changed your lifestyle to accommodate caring for your dog/cat? Are you afraid to stay out too long in the evening because you're worried about your pet? Has it been a while since you've taken a vacation because you don't trust anyone to take proper care of your beloved dog? When you must go away—say, on business—are you distracted and feel you must check in with your pet sitter regularly, even obsessively?
5. How about finances? Has the cost of your pet's treatment put a strain on your budget and, therefore, on you? Has it figured into your decision to treat or not to treat? Have you felt compelled to "shop around" for vets based on price, and then worry that you might "get what you pay for"?

Quality of your life at this time is about achieving balance, and to do that you must be honest with yourself. Nobody said it was going to be easy, and of course you'll have your bad days, but if caring for your sick dog is becoming more of a burden than a labor of love, you need to acknowledge that so that you can better determine how to proceed.

We are fortunate, indeed, to be able to extend the time we spend with these remarkable companions. And the longer we spend with our dogs, the stronger the bond between us grows. But the stronger the bond grows, the more difficult it becomes to "let go"—or to even think about it. But think about it we must, if we are to spare our dogs and ourselves greater distress. If we prepare ourselves for the inevitable end of this beautiful friendship, our reward will be knowing we "did right by our dog," as she deserved, and right by ourselves, as we too deserve.

Think About It

What's the best way to prepare yourself? First, just by thinking about it—not pushing "those" thoughts away when they come. It may help to think of this as an anticipatory grief period. A lot has been written and discussed about the five stages of grief—denial, anger, bargaining, depression, and acceptance—following the death of a loved one, but many of us often go through these stages *before* the loved one dies. In particular, many pet owners are prone to the first stage, denial. As discussed in Chapter 2, a common mistake pet owners make is to "not see" signs from their dogs that something is wrong. Sometimes not seeing is a function of not paying attention, but it might also be a function of *not wanting to see,* or—you guessed it—denial. We know our dog is at the end of her lifespan; we know she won't live forever. But still we may refuse to acknowledge those facts in our "heart of hearts." We hang on, literally, for dear life. You will have to find the way that works best for you to break through the denial.

Talk About It

For many people, it helps to talk to others, those who know us and know our dog and who understand the importance of this relationship in our lives. Those who have gone through the process themselves are particularly helpful. Your vet may be able to put you in touch with another client who is willing to share his or her letting-go process in an effort to help you through your own.

Another option is to join an online chat group. Because of the "distance" conferred by the technology, this may be an easier venue in which to communicate at this time—you can come and go as you please and participate as much or as little as you wish. Check out: www.pethobbyist.com and www.doghobbyist.com/chat. Or type in search parameters such as "dog chat room" or "pet chat room," and you'll find many more choices.

Consult with Your Vet

It's always a good idea to keep your vet in the loop, not just about your dog's health but your state of mind as well. That is the only way he or she can properly advise you at this difficult time. Your vet can't make your decision for you, but he or she can ease the way for you. You might want to make an appointment with your vet for the express purpose of determining when to cease active treatment, especially if your dog is terminally ill. Ironically, this has been made more difficult by the very science and technology that gave our aging dogs quality lives for so long. Many treatment protocols can be continued for extended periods of time, so the question that must be asked is, At what value? At some point, we are, as Dr. Goldston said, prolonging dying, not meaningful living.

You may even want to consider seeking a second opinion at this juncture, because veterinarians, too, become emotionally invested in the care of their patients and sometimes have trouble acknowledging the true circumstances of a situation, thus wanting to continue making heroic attempts at cure.

Provide Hospice Care

"When the goal of treatment begins to shift from curing illness to providing comfort, it is time to consider hospice." That's the guideline of the American Association of Human-Animal Bond Veterinarians (AAHABV). A logical outgrowth of the modern human hospice movement, which began in the 1970s, veterinary hospice care is fast becoming a widely recommended and implemented end-of-life care program for terminally ill and seriously disabled companion animals.

In its "Senior Care Guidelines for Dogs and Cats," the American Animal Hospital Association cites the American Veterinary Medical Association (AVMA) definition of veterinary hospice care as: "giving clients time to make decisions regarding a terminal companion animal and to prepare for [its] pending death," while always taking into consideration the comfort of the animal. The AAHABV defines it as a system that "provides compassionate comfort care to patients at the end of their lives and also supports their families in the bereavement process." To that end, it includes "comprehensive nursing care as well as psychosocial and spiritual care for the patient and the family."

Who's Who in Pet Health Care: American Association of Human-Animal Bond Veterinarians (AAHABV)

The threefold mission of the AAHABV is to "further veterinary awareness, scientific progress, and educational opportunities in the area of the human-animal bond; to encourage veterinary participation in human-animal bond activities with related organizations and disciplines; and to explore the potential for establishing a veterinary specialty in the area of human-animal bond." For more on this organization in general, and its approach to veterinary hospice specifically, go to http://aahabv.org.

Many people unfamiliar with the concept of hospice care, whether human or animal, mistakenly think of hospice as a place, such as a hospital or nursing home. In fact, hospice care is given primarily in the patient's home; and for animals this is almost always the case. Hospice care (also commonly referred to as *palliative* care) for a companion animal is based on the individual's specific requirements. Depending on your dog's disease or illness and age, according to the AAHA, hospice care for your dog might include:

- Outpatient/home care
- Pain management
- Easy access to food, water, and "bathroom" facilities
- Wound management
- A stable and consistent environment

- Good hygiene and sanitation
- Clean bedding and padding
- Mental stimulation

In addition, nutritional maintenance (balancing a therapeutic diet while maintaining caloric intake) is "paramount" for a dog receiving hospice care, says the AAHA.

Typically, home visits by your veterinarian or a member of his or her staff are also recommended as part of the program, whenever possible. During this time, your vet should also conduct what is essentially a risk-benefit analysis of any medications and treatments still being provided. Again, the goal is to sustain good quality of life, not prolong dying.

The objective of hospice care is, ultimately, a peaceful death for your dog, whether by euthanasia or natural causes. Thus, as important as meeting the AAHA guidelines for providing that care is to focus on giving your dog regular doses of love and attention throughout this period.

To Learn More About Hospice Care . . .

Go to www.pethospice.org. This is the Web site of the Nikki Hospice Foundation for Pets, the first official organization committed to providing hospice care for terminally ill or dying companion animals. Here you'll find in-depth FAQs about the foundation, as well as hospice care in general, and a number of links related to pet loss.

SUMMARY

This chapter raised a number of questions, questions difficult to answer because they require us to interpret quality of life for our dog, who is coming to the end of her life. At the same time we are trying to do what's best for our dog, we often are consumed with feelings of confusion and conflict. We may seesaw between the urge to ease our dog's passing, when we know she is suffering, and the temptation to do whatever it takes at whatever cost to keep our dog alive for just a little while longer. It is at this time we must answer the call to return the unconditional and unselfish love our dogs have given us throughout their lives with us: we must let go. In the next chapter, we talk about the most difficult aspect of caring for an aging dog: deciding it is time to euthanize her.

KEY PET POINTS

- Tune in to clues from your dog that her quality of life may be in jeopardy, and follow those clues.
- Familiarize yourself with pain behaviors, just as you learned to recognize signs of illness.
- Work closely with your vet in managing your dog's pain treatments and/or therapies. Continuous monitoring is essential.
- Consult with your vet about the feasibility of providing hospice care for your dog, while preparing yourself for the heart-wrenching effort of letting go.

CHAPTER 9

Farewell, Friend: Coming to Terms with End of Life

It's unclear when the euphemism "put to sleep" came into widespread use as the alternative for euthanizing companion animals. Perhaps it was coined to soothe the breaking hearts of so many pet owners who hope and pray their ailing pets will die peacefully in their sleep. We want this most difficult decision made for us. We want no doubt that the time is right to say good-bye. Like Watson's owner, (see "Watson's Story" in Chapter 5), we

may find ourselves looking toward the heavens and saying, "Please don't make me do your job for you." But for most of us, this will be our job, the last we will have to do for our aged and ailing dogs. And we will be expected to carry out this final act of care even as we are in the throes of grief. Nothing could be more painful.

MAKING THE DECISION TO EUTHANIZE

There is no way to ease the anguish caused by the impending death of a beloved dog, but by addressing all the issues involved in advance, it is possible to ease the passage, so that the loss is not preceded, and so complicated, by feelings of panic, misunderstanding, and uncertainty.

The Good Death

Though some dogs do, of course, pass peacefully in their sleep, this is not the norm today. The same advances in veterinary medicine that enable us to keep our dogs alive longer, even in the face of serious illness and disease, also force us to make the decision when to stop taking heroic measures—we must acknowledge when we are prolonging dying. Dr. Goldston says that the single gravest misconception pet owners have about their pets is that they will die peacefully, at home, in their sleep. Euthanasia, Greek for "good death," is the humane option for most pet owners.

Many people have mixed feelings about euthanasia, and few make the decision easily, and many suffer guilt afterward. You may find yourself thinking such things as, "This goes against nature— I'm killing my dog." But if you consider that all the advanced treatments your dog received—surgeries, medications, and so on—kept him alive longer than nature intended, you may be able to realize that euthanasia is more a decision to stop keeping your dog alive artificially.

You may also feel you're "giving up," and maybe too soon. Shouldn't you get another opinion, try another treatment, research other options? The best way to address this feeling is in close consult with your veterinarian. In its "Senior Care Guidelines for Dogs and Cats," the American Animal Hospital Association (AAHA) recommends that vets aid their clients in "assessing their animal's welfare and in making an ethical decision" by considering the "five freedoms," as established by the London-based Farm Animal Advisory Council (FAWC). These include:

- Freedom from hunger and thirst
- Freedom from discomfort
- Freedom from pain, injury, and disease

- Freedom from fear and distress
- Freedom to express normal behavior

So, for example, critical decision points for you may be when your dog has trouble breathing, no longer eats or drinks enough to sustain himself, cannot get comfortable when he tries to rest or sleep, or shrinks from your touch because he is in pain.

In addition to helping clients evaluate their pet's condition, vets also often ask them in advance about their wishes regarding the euthanasia process and aftercare. By doing this, pet owners do not have to make these difficult decisions during a period of emotional duress or crisis (for example, if their dog suddenly and dramatically takes a turn for the worse). If your vet does not request this information from you in advance, you can take the initiative yourself, after considering the following issues:

- Where would you prefer the procedure take place: at home or in the vet's office/veterinary hospital?
- Do you want to be present during and/or after the procedure?
- Do you want others to attend as well (a friend, family members, children)?
- Do you plan to have your dog's body buried or cremated?

Let's delve into each of these issues.

Location

A lot of pet owners want their dog euthanized at home, for a variety of reasons:

- It is less stressful for the dog, especially if he is very ill and/or large, hence difficult to transport at this stage.
- They want their dog to have all the comforts of home at this difficult time.

- Home ensures privacy for you and anyone else who will be present, and enables you and others to give free rein to your emotions.

But before you choose this option, consider carefully whether having your dog euthanized at home might make the grieving process more difficult for you (and your family) later, because you will be constantly reminded that here is where he died. You should also find out, in advance, whether your vet does home euthanasia. If not, and you're sure this is what you want to do, you can find one who does by logging on to www.athomevet.org, the Web site for the American Association of Housecall Veterinarians.

All that said, euthanizing your dog in your vet's office or a hospital need not be cold and impersonal. You can bring your dog's favorite blanket, an article of your own clothing you've worn (your smell will comfort him), or a favorite toy. And vets today go out of their way to make this time as stress-free as possible, typically allowing their clients as much privacy and time before and after the procedure as they need. Vets and their staff know only too well what you are going through and are as compassionate as they are professional, ensuring that your dog has not only the safest treatment, but the kindest as well.

Your Role

Will you be there? Yes, say many pet owners! No matter how difficult, they feel they want to be—must be—there for their dogs, to give them comfort and security. It may be a point of honor as well, a desire to pay homage to the unmatched companionship their dogs gave to them, to return the favor. For other people, however, seeing their dog die is simply too traumatic, and they fear they will only upset their dog by being so distraught in his presence. Some ask a surrogate to stand in for them, someone who knows them and/or their dog well and understands why they cannot bear to be in the room at that time. No judgment is attached to this decision—remember, it's about you, too.

If your dog is the family dog, others in his clan (including other pets) may also want to be present during the euthanasia. If you have decided to have the procedure done at home, this should be no problem. If, on the other hand, it will take place in your vet's office, check in advance whether this is possible. First, some vets do not allow very young children (five years or younger) or other animals to be present during euthanasia; second, too many people crowded into a small treatment room may only add stress to the situation—and to your dog.

Aftercare

For so long that living, breathing bundle of joy seemed more a spirit, a character, a personality, which just happened to be wrapped in fur and come to earth on four legs. Now you must think about his body, separate from that spirit. If you do no other planning before your dog dies, decide in advance what you want done with your dog's remains, for you will not want to think about this in the immediate aftermath of his death.

The two major options are burial and cremation, and within each of those choices are two secondary options.

BURIAL

If you decide you want to bury your dog, how you go about it will depend on where you live. Many people with their own homes choose to situate their dog's grave in their yard—his yard. If this is your inclination, two cautions to be aware of:

- First, though your home is your private property, you may be prohibited by local laws from burying your dog there, so be sure to check this in advance. Even if it is allowed, there may be requirements as to the depth of the grave, for health reasons.

- Second, consider how you will feel if you one day move from this residence and must leave your dog's remains behind.

The second burial option is a pet cemetery. These exist now throughout the United States, though you may have to go some distance from your local area to find one. The advantages to this option are that there is no question you will be within the scope of the law; your dog's grave site will be cared for and undisturbed; and you can visit the site as you would any departed family members. Interment at a pet cemetery will cost more, however; and, as with home burial, if you should one day leave the area, you leave your dog behind.

Hallowed Ground

For more information on pet cemeteries, or to find one in your area, go to the International Association of Pet Cemeteries and Crematories Web site, www.iaopc.com, or to Moira Allen's Pet Loss Support Web site, www.pet-loss.net. Both also have links to all areas of pet-loss support.

CREMATION

Cremation is the preference for many pet owners these days, especially urban dwellers. You can choose group cremation or individual cremation, and you will base your decision on whether you want your dog's ashes returned to you. Cost may also be a consideration, as group cremation is less expensive.

- If you choose group cremation, following your dog's death, generally you will leave his body with your vet, who will take care of transporting his body to a pet crematorium or animal shelter for the process.
- If you choose individual cremation, you will still leave your dog's

body with your vet, who will ensure it is handled individually and returned to you—usually in an appropriate box or other container. Once your dog's remains have been returned to you, you may want to put them in a more meaningful or decorative urn and place it appropriately in your home. Or you may want to scatter his ashes, or bury them, in one of his favorite spots.

THE CONCLUSION OF CASEY'S STORY: FINAL ACT OF CARE

By the time Casey was twelve, we were treating several serious chronic conditions. Then came the day he couldn't get up. An MRI and spinal fluid analysis revealed a lesion on his brain. He responded well, but slowly, over the next few weeks to a steroidal anti-inflammatory, and we adjusted his routine to compensate (shorter walks on level ground, for example) until he was back to his usual strength. But the medication he had to take for the rest of his life was  not without side effects. When Casey was about thirteen, a short cough woke me up one morning about 3:30. After about a week of this happening every day at the same time, an ultrasound was performed, which confirmed a diagnosis of chronic obstructive pulmonary disease (COPD). More medication, also for the rest of his life.

At one point, for several months, Casey was taking so many medications and supplements that we prepared a spreadsheet, and a kitchen timer became our best friend! We also learned, by reviewing every medication and supplement with every doctor involved in Casey's treatment, that two of the medications had the potential for serious interaction effects. The two specialists involved researched options and made adjustments.

Probably the most important lesson we learned from taking care of Casey was the absolute necessity of finding the right veterinarians and specialists and developing trusting, supportive relationships with them. They were all partners with us in Casey's care, responding to phone calls and e-mails promptly; and—very important—they were all willing to talk to one another.

As Casey aged, we made changes to accommodate his changing needs and the effects of some of the medication. We researched foods to determine a healthy diet and periodically reviewed the supplements he was taking. And when he began to lose his hearing, we began using hand signals as well as voice signals to communicate with him. During his last years, he began needing to relieve himself during the night. We already were carrying him up and down stairs to our bedroom at night to reduce stress on his arthritic joints, but it was too inconvenient to do it during the night. Fortunately, he always went to the same spot to urinate—appropriately, the main bathroom. So we lined the floor there with puppy pads and changed them in the morning.

Even with all the medical issues, treatments, and ongoing medications, for a long while, Casey had a good quality of life. He ate well, loved his treats, enjoyed going for short walks, liked to snuggle and be petted, and enjoyed people—until one day in July 2003, when he wouldn't eat his regular food, became very lethargic, and looked very sad. Tests revealed untreatable liver cancer. The night following that diagnosis, I slept on the floor with Casey. He would sleep with my arm draped over him for an hour or so, get up and pace the length of the hall, come back and sleep again, over and over all night. The next morning, after we carried him downstairs, he walked over in front of the door leading into the garage and lay down. He wouldn't take anything by mouth, and his eyes were dull and half shut. I laid down next to him, petted him, and spoke softly to him until the vet's office opened. Wrapped in one of his comforters and nestled in my husband's arms, we took him in, knowing that he wouldn't be coming home. The last thing our beloved puppy saw was my face and the last thing he felt was my husband's hand gently lying on his side.

UNDERSTANDING THE PROCEDURE

Each of us facing a frightening or upsetting situation handles it in our own way. Some of us find that knowing as much as possible about what will happen calms our fears; for others, the less we know, the better. You know yourself what level of knowledge empowers you and what kind just makes you feel worse, especially when it comes to medical procedures. So it is with the process of euthanasia. You might want to understand exactly what will happen to your dog, or you may cringe at the mention of any specifics. Therefore, this section only briefly describes the procedure. If you think that a more comprehensive understanding of euthanasia will help give you peace of mind, as part of your advance planning, ask your vet to explain in as much detail as you want what your dog will experience.

Procedural Variations

Though the procedure described here is typical, each vet will have his or her own euthanasia protocol, depending in part where you have chosen to have it done.

Most vets today administer a sedative or tranquilizer prior to the euthanasia drug, sometimes in pill form, but more commonly as an injection under the skin, like a vaccination. This calms your dog quickly—and perhaps you, too, just seeing your dog relax. (At this point, you may want a few minutes alone with your dog, to say good-bye.) Next, your vet will insert an intravenous (IV) catheter in one of your dog's veins (often in a back leg). If your vet did not already sedate your dog, he or she may do so now, through the IV catheter and syringe. When you're ready (most vets ask), the vet will administer the euthanasia drug, which is an overdose of a barbiturate. (If you have chosen to have the procedure done at home, the vet may use only a needle and syringe.) Most pet owners who have decided to stay with their dog at this time will gently stroke their dogs and speak softly to them.

Very quickly it will be over. Your dog's head may droop or slowly fall over, and your vet will check for a heartbeat to confirm he is gone.

Whether at home or at your vet's office, you will probably want to spend a few minutes—or more—with your dog after he has died. Take all the time you need; it is not easy to step away, especially as it will feel like you are leaving a big piece of your heart behind.

You will probably not be able to think straight initially, and this is why it is so important to have decided in advance how you will

Prepare Yourself

I n most cases, dying from euthanasia will seem just like a gentle
release of tension, but you should also be aware of the following:

- Your dog's eyes will *not* shut when he dies.
- Your dog's body may twitch, his heart may beat for a couple of
  seconds after he has stopped breathing, and you may hear
  sounds, such as sighing.
- There may be a release of your dog's bladder and bowels, so
  if you plan to hold your dog in your arms or lap while he is
  euthanized, cover yourself first with a towel or blanket.

handle your dog's body. If you have decided to cremate your dog, usually your vet will take care of transporting the body to the pet crematorium; if you have decided for a burial in a pet cemetery, in general
they will pick up your dog; and if you have decided to bury your dog
on your own property, his body will remain with you.

COPING WITH THE LOSS OF YOUR DOG

Dogs only break your heart once, but it's a compound fracture, one
that is painful and slow to heal. Their very absence is a kind of presence. Everywhere they were, you look for them, sense them, see
them. Out of the corner of your eye, you catch a flash of movement;
you turn quickly to look, expecting to see him there, only to realize your eyes were playing tricks on you. When you get up from
your favorite chair, you automatically step over where your dog
always used to lie; now it seems you are stepping into space.

And you never know when it's going to rise up, this groundswell
of emotion for your absent friend. You may prepare yourself for it
as you walk through the door at night knowing he won't be there
to greet you, tail thumping in time to your pats on his head; or in
the morning as you wait for your coffee to brew, your hands are

uncomfortably idle when they should be filling his bowl, refreshing his water, so you fuss with some unnecessary chore or other. But even worse, it comes when you least expect it. You walk into a meeting with a new client, in full professional garb, with attitude to match, sure of yourself and your presentation. Then, suddenly, you see on the client's desk, a picture of him with his children and their dog—a dog not really like yours at all, yet your eyes fill, threatening to spill over. Or you're watching a movie on TV that has nothing to do with dogs, or even animals, but it's about loss, and suddenly you're in a puddle of tears.

Grief is like that: it's sneaky and erratic, coming and going, and coming back again. It has no time frame; it keeps no schedule. There is little you can do except "go with the flow," and accept that whatever you are feeling, whenever, wherever, is the way it has to be for you. What it doesn't have to be for you is lonely. No matter what your circumstance or living situation, you do not have to grieve alone—unless, of course, that's the way you choose, the way that's best for you. But most people, at least at some point during the grief process, feel the need to talk, to share, to just be, with someone else.

Gone are the days when people felt they had to keep the loss of a beloved pet to themselves, for fear of hearing such remarks as, "It's only a dog; if you feel that bad, just get another one." Though such insensitivity still exists, and there will be times and situations when you won't feel comfortable mentioning your loss and grief, in general, the human-animal bond is recognized as one of the most intense and important to people, and its severing by the death of a pet is a well-understood cause of grief and depression.

You've no doubt heard the experience of grief described as a process, defined by Elisabeth Kubler-Ross in her now-classic book, *On Death and Dying* (first published in 1975), as occurring in five stages: denial, anger, bargaining, depression, and acceptance. But this is not necessarily a neat sequential process, progressing from stage one to stage five and then you're done and ready to move on.

Rather, it can be quite messy and long lasting, and so very disturbing and disruptive. You may zig and zag between the stages, one day angry at your dog for leaving you, or at your vet because there was nothing else she could do; the next day, you wake relieved that your dog is no longer suffering and that you are no longer stressed from the worry and the effort of caring for him, and you accept that you did all that you could; three days later, you're sunk so deeply in sadness you can't see your way out. And so it goes. And go it eventually does. Until then, you may need a helping hand—or heart—to see you through.

Fortunately, today, pet-loss grief counseling is widely available. And this is no one-size-fits-all support; it is as highly individualized as the grief process itself. You can join a group, get one-on-one counseling, talk on the phone, connect online, or any combination, to suit your personality, your schedule, and your emotional state. In short, help is there—everywhere—when and where you need it.

Pet-Loss Hotlines

Pet-loss hotlines are call-in programs, staffed by volunteers or professionals or, in the case of veterinary school hotlines, by students. Most of the lines have limited call-in hours, usually in the evenings—typically between 5 or 6 and 9 or 10 p.m. Some of the best known are given here, but this list is far from comprehensive. Note that some of these numbers are main switchboards, so you may need to ask to be connected to the pet bereavement hotline. And note that most of the phone numbers will mean a long-distance charge if you're out of the area, so it will be worth your while to call your local humane organization for a hotline in your community; or go to www.aplb.org, the Web site of the Association for Pet Loss and Bereavement (APLB).

University of California-Davis Pet Loss Support Hotline: 800-565-1526 or 530-752-3602

Helping Children Cope with Pet Loss

Part of your own grieving process may be to help other members of your family, especially young children, face the death of the family dog.

When a dearly loved dog dies, it is often a young child's first experience with death, and so must be addressed carefully. The child's age and level of maturity, as well as his or her state of mind, must be considered, but generally, "honesty is the best policy," as is a straightforward approach. Children are remarkably astute and often can sense what's *not* being said; and they're also very literal, so phrases like "putting the dog to sleep" may just confuse a child who may later wonder why the dog can't just "wake up."

It often helps children to understand the finality of death by memorializing their dog in some way—putting flowers on a grave, or planting a tree or bush in the dog's name, for example. They should also be encouraged to express their feelings through drawing, writing, and, of course, talking. Another very effective way to broach the subject is through reading. Four titles worth reviewing for appropriateness to your child or children are: *When a Pet Dies* by Fred Rogers (PaperStar Books, Putnam & Grosset Group, 1998); *Sad Isn't Bad: A Good-Grief Guidebook for Kids Dealing with Loss*, written by Michaelene Mundy and illustrated by Robert W. Alley (Abbey Press, 1998); *I'll Always Love You* by Hans Wilhelm (Crown Books for Young Readers, 1985); and *Dog Heaven*, by Cynthia Rylant (Blue Sky Press, 1995).

Keep a close eye on your children at this time, watching for signs of extreme or prolonged distress—loss of appetite, depression, anger, sleeping problems, and so on. In such cases, you may need to find professional help.

University of California-Davis Pet Loss Support Hotline:
800-565-1526 or 530-752-3602
Tufts University, Cummings School of Veterinary Medicine:
508-839-5302
Cornell University Pet Loss Support Hotline: 607-253-3932
Chicago Veterinary Medical Association: 630-325-1600
Colorado State University Veterinary Teaching Hospital/Argus
Institute: 970-297-1242

Note:

You don't have to wait until your dog has died to seek help. If you're having a difficult time making the decision to euthanize or facing your dog's impending death, connect with someone beforehand to get the support you need.

Online Chat Rooms

As noted in Chapter 8, an increasingly popular venue for talking about pet loss, and finding and giving support, is online. Anytime of the day or night, you can log on and find a kindred spirit. Just type "pet loss chat" into your search engine and you'll find hundreds of choices. It's a good idea to spend some time reading through a few of these before you begin to participate, however, to ensure that you find a group you're comfortable interacting with.

Grief Counseling

For many of us, there's just no substitute for personal, face-to-face interaction, especially when we're having a hard time coping with loss. Grief counselors (generally, psychologists or social workers), some specializing in pet loss, will meet with you one-on-one or give you the opportunity to participate in group sessions as well (you may want to do both). Most humane organizations, shelters, and some veterinary hospitals and clinics also sponsor support groups.

Animals Know Loss, Too

I f yours is a multipet household, be aware that other dogs or cats may feel the loss of the missing dog, too, especially if they were closely bonded. The sudden occurrence of behavior problems following the death of your dog is the typical sign—wailing, loss of housebreaking, and loss of appetite. In most cases, just spending time with your other pets, and adhering to their normal routine, will comfort and settle them in short order.

The best way to find a grief counselor or support group is through a personal recommendation. Your vet surely will be able to supply you with one or more names; ask friends, family, and other dog owners, as well. Or, for a state guide to pet support groups and counselors, check out Moira Anderson Allen's excellent Pet Loss Support Web site, www.pet-loss.com.

Self-Care

During the grieving process, probably no form of support is more important than the support you give yourself. Take time off if you need it. If you think—or know—your employer won't accommodate a pet bereavement period, consider calling in sick—you are, after all, sick at heart. Then take care of yourself: get plenty of rest and eat right. Exercise, too; it will help you sleep.

Keep good company, with people who will understand what you're going through. Stay away from anyone from the "it's just a dog" school of thought. Or, if you prefer, spend quality time with yourself: go to the movies, read, rearrange the furniture—do whatever it takes to soothe your aching heart.

Finally, take heart: the day will come when you begin to notice that when you think about your absent friend, you're smiling instead of crying. The healing has begun.

SUMMARY

The death of a loved one is a wound, for which there is no salve or bandage except time. But never does time creep so slowly as when we wait for it to apply its healing hands. To help pass this time, we may seek the comfort and compassion of those who understand our bereavement; but in the end, we each must simply live through it.

KEY PET POINTS

- As much as you might wish it otherwise, recognize that you probably will have to decide to euthanize your dog so that he doesn't suffer unnecessarily. And that will be the last, best gift you can give him.
- Learn from your vet what to expect as your dog's disease or illness progresses, to help you make the decision when to cease treatment. Your vet cannot and will not decide for you, but he or she will give you guidance.
- So that you do not suffer unnecessarily, consider in advance the details of the euthanasia procedure and aftercare.
- Grieve, as you must, but know that you are not alone and that help is available to you in many forms and from many sources.

Epilogue

It was bound to happen, I suppose—though without realizing it I had been crossing my fingers that it wouldn't. While writing this book, one of the dogs I had come to know—not "in person," but in spirit—died.

It was on a Saturday morning when a friend called, sobbing, to tell me that Nilla, her Labrador retriever, had been diagnosed with bone cancer in her shoulder, and would have to be euthanized. Unsuspectingly the tumor had grown, high above the only actual sign of a problem, in Nilla's ankle, which had been diagnosed as a minor case of arthritis. A poster child for the remarkable capability of the dog to hide pain and weakness, Nilla had given no indication of the larger, looming problem, until the day before, when she took one wrong step and could no longer hide her extreme discomfort.

Nilla, on recycling duty.

My friend had called from the airport, on her way to visit her mother, a trip it was too late to cancel. So the loss was doubly felt: she would lose her dog and could not be at her husband's side to say good-bye to Nilla.

There are no happy endings in the tale of care for the senior dog. But there can be peaceful endings—and, of course, happy memories. And then there are new beginnings.

Your dog cannot be replaced. Period. But your relationship with her has expanded your capacity to love, and one day sooner or later—perhaps on the first day you find yourself laughing instead of crying when your think of your dog—you may find yourself wanting to share that love and care with another dog. Few people who have been the object of a dog's unique brand of affection ever want to live without it again. When this might happen for you, however, is as personal as the grief you've been experiencing. There are those pet owners who plan right away to welcome another dog into their homes and hearts—some even begin planning for the new addition to the family before their senior dog dies. This is their way of helping to cope with the impending loss. Others wait weeks, months, even longer. There is no right time—except the right time for you.

The best guideline here, and one that you've read repeatedly in this book, is to trust your instincts. You'll find you "just happen" to be at the mall when the pet superstore there is having its weekly adoption day. Or you'll starting turning immediately to the classifieds in the paper "just to see" what's available. Maybe you'll turn down the street where you know you can see through the window at the local animal shelter's adoption department. You may not even be aware you're looking, or you'll tell yourself you are "*just* looking." Then before you know it, a dog picks you out.

That's usually the way it happens: we think we pick them, but most often it's the other way around. They know how to trust their instincts, and they never doubt them. Their keen sense of smell includes having a nose for who is right for them. One day it will be you—you lucky dog!

Resources

General Information

BOOKS:

ASPCA Complete Dog Care Manual, by Bruce Fogle (DK Adult, 1993).

Dog Owner's Home Veterinary Handbook, by James M. Giffin (Howell Book House, 2000).

First Aid for Dogs: What to Do When Emergencies Happen, by Bruce Fogle (Penguin, 1997).

The Pill Book Guide to Medication for Your Dog and Cat, by Kate Roby and Lenny Southam (Bantam, 1998).

UC Davis Book of Dogs: The Complete Medical Reference Guide for Dogs and Puppies, by Mordecai Siegal (University of California at Davis, 1995).

WEB SITES

Merck Veterinary Manual Online: www.merckvetmanual.com/mvm/index.jsp

VeterinaryPartner.com: www.veterinarypartner.com

Humane Organizations

American Society for the Prevention of Cruelty to Animals (ASPCA): 212-876-7700, Ext 4650; www.aspca.org

Humane Society of the United States (HSUS): 202-452-1100; www.hsus.org

San Francisco Society for the Prevention of Cruelty to Animals (SFSPCA): 415-554-3000; www.sfspca.org

Professional Veterinary Organizations

American Animal Hospital Association (AAHA): 303-986-2800; ww.aahanet.org

Note: Though primarily for practitioners, the AAHA Web site is a good source of background on the profession for laypersons. Also, go to the association's www.healthypet.com Web site for guidelines and information on aging pets, where you can request a copy of "Senior Moments," a concise brochure on health care for the older pet.

American Association of Human-Animal Bond Veterinarians (AAHABV): http://aahabv.org

American Holistic Veterinary Medical Association (AHVMA): 410-569-0795; www.ahvma.org

American Veterinary Dental College: 215-573-8135; www.avdc.org

American Veterinary Medical Association (AVMA): 800-248-2862; www.avma.org

Note: The AVMA site is primarily for members, but public information is available by clicking on the Care for Animals and News links.

International Veterinary Academy of Pain Management (IVAPM): 970-297-1257; www.cvmbs.colostate.edu/ivapm

Note: View the online video, "Is My Dog in Pain?"

Professional Pet-Related Organizations

American Kennel Club: www.akc.org

Association of American Feed Control Officials: www.aafco.org

Pet Food Institute (PFI): www.petfoodinstitute.org

U.S. Food and Drug Administration Center for Veterinary Medicine: www.fda.gov/cvm

American Pet Products Manufacturer's Association (APPMA): www.appma.org

Purina Pet Institute: www.purina.com/institute

Pet Supply Companies

Note: Online shoppers for pet supplies and services of all kinds should go to www.bhejei.co/mailorder.htm, which has lengthy lists of sources in all categories of pet care.

GENERAL

Drs Fosters & Smith: www.drsfostersmith.com

Senior Pet Products.com: www.seniorpetproducts.com

MOBILITY AIDS

K-9 Cart Company: www.k9carts.com

Bottom's Up Leash: www.bottomsupleash.com

Dewey's Wheelchairs for Dogs: www.wheelchairsfordogs.com

Eddie's Wheels: www.eddieswheels.com

Drs. Foster & Smith: www.drsfostersmith.com

DogRamp.com: www.dogramp.com

Pet Insurance and Wellness Programs

Note: These listings are intended only as places to start your research, not as recommendations. The pet insurance industry is still developing, and many of these companies are new on the scene. In all cases, due diligence is required: read the fine print, especially as it applies to older pets and preexisting conditions.

INSURANCE
Veterinary Pet Insurance (the oldest)
Phone: 800-872-7387
Web site: www.petinsurance.com

PetCare Pet Insurance
Phone: 866-373-7387
Web site: www.petcarepals.com

Petshealth Care Plan
Phone: 800-807-6724
Web site: www.petshealthplan.com

Premier Pet Insurance
Phone: 877-774-2273
Web site: www.ppins.com

TruePaws Family Pet Insurance Company
Phone: 877-832-6195
Web site: www.truepaws.com

WELLNESS PROGRAMS
Pet Assure
Phone: 888-789-7387
Web site: www.petassure.com

Optimum Wellness Plan
Phone: 866-277-7387
www.petsmart.com/banfield/index.shtml

Pet-Food Cookbooks

Dr. Pitcairn's New Complete Guide to Natural Health for Dogs and Cats, by Richard H. Pitcairn, DVM (Rodale Books, 2005).

The Good Food Cookbook for Dogs: 50 Home-Cooked Recipes for the Health and Happiness of Your Canine Companion, by Donna Twichell Roberts (Quarry Books, 2004).

Better Food for Dogs: A Complete Cookbook and Nutrition Guide, by David Basin and Jennifer Ashton (Robert Rose, 2002).

Alternative Veterinary Medicine Information

Alternatives for Animals: www.alternativesforanimals.com
American Holistic Veterinary Medical Association: www.ahvma.org

Canine Cancer Information
Canine Cancer Awareness: www.caninecancerawareness.org
Veterinary Cancer Society: www.veterinarycancersociety.org
Perseus Foundation: www.perseusfoundation.org

Pain Management Information
Pfizer Animal Health Division: www.Pfizer.com
Veterinary Academy of Pain Management at Colorado State University of
Veterinary Medicine: www.cvmbs.colostate.edu/ivapm

Pet Hospice Information
Nikki Hospice Foundation for Pets: www.pethospice.org

Pet Meds Online
National Association of Boards of Pharmacy (NABP): www.nabp.net; or call
847-698-6227
> *Note: Before ordering any of your pet's medicines online, contact the NABP to
> confirm that the pharmacy is licensed and in good standing.*

Internet Pets: www.internetpets.com
Drs. Foster & Smith: www.drsfostersmith.com
Pet Med Express: www.petmedexpress.com

Pet Cemeteries
Moira Allen's Pet Loss Support Web site: www.pet-loss.net
International Association of Pet Cemeteries site: www.iaopc.com
Note: Both these sites also have links to all areas of pet-loss support.

Pet-Loss Support
GENERAL
Association for Pet Loss and Bereavement (APLB): www.aplb.org

SUPPORT HOTLINES
University of California-Davis: 509-335-5704 or 800-565-1526
Tufts University: 508-839-5302
Cornell University: 607-253-3932
The Delta Society: 619-320-3298
Chicago Veterinary Medicine Association: 630-603-3994
Colorado State University Veterinary Teaching Hospital: 970-491-1242

ONLINE CHAT ROOMS
www.chat.pethobbyist.com
www.doghobbyist.com/chat

BOOKS

The Loss of a Pet, 3rd edition, by Wallace Sife (John Wiley & Sons, 2005).

BOOKS FOR CHILDREN

When a Pet Dies, by Fred Rogers (Penguin Books for Young Readers, 1998).

Sad Isn't Bad: A Good-Grief Guidebook for Kids Dealing with Loss, written by Michaelene Mundy and illustrated by Robert W. Alley (Abbey Press Printing and Publishing, 1998).

I'll Always Love You, by Hans Wilhelm (Crown Books for Young Readers, 1998).

Dog Heaven, by Cynthia Rylant (Blue Sky Press, 1995).

Poison Control

ASPCA Poison Control Center: 888-426-443

Senior Citizen-Pet Matchup Programs

Pets for the Elderly (PEF): www.petsfortheelderly.org; or call 866-849-3598

Partnering Animals with Seniors (P. A. W. S.): www.azhumane.org

Miscellaneous Web Sites

www.athomevet.org: The Web site of the American Association of Housecall Veterinarians, where you can find a vet in your area who makes house calls.

http://animalbehaviorcounselors.org: Association of Companion Animal Behavior Counselors (ACABC)

www.barfworld.com: For information on the raw diet, Biologically Appropriate Raw Food (BARF).

www.bravorawdiet.com: For information on the raw diet, Bravo.

www.dogpark.com: To find a dog park in your area or to learn how to start one.

www.handicappedpets.com: To find rehabilitation facilities, by state.

www.healthradionetwork.com: Dr. Marty Becker's weekly radio program, "Top Vets Talk Pets."

www.library.uiuc.edu/vex/vetdocs/abbreviation.htm: Log on here to help decipher those mysterious abbreviations and acronyms.

www.medipet.com: Ready-made first-aid kits.

www.npwm.com: For information on National Pet Wellness Month.

www.Pets911.com: Enter your zip code to find animal shelters, agencies, and other animal care organizations in your community.

www.purina.com/dogs/nutrition: To view the Body Condition System, for determining obesity.

Index

CARING
FOR YOUR
AGING DOG